D1156521

HILTON HEAD

A Sea Island Chronicle

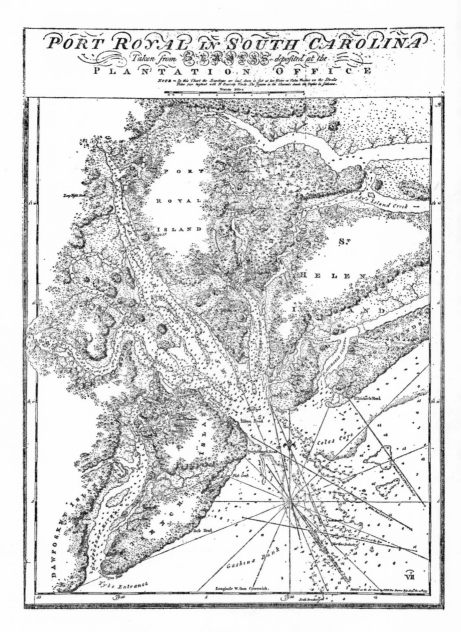

Published as the Act directs By J. F. W. DesBarres, Esq. Aug. 10th, 1777. — *Original in Honey Horn Big House.*

HILTON HEAD

A SEA ISLAND
CHRONICLE

by VIRGINIA C. HOLMGREN

Hilton Head Island Publishing Company
HILTON HEAD ISLAND, S. C. 29928

TABLE
OF CONTENTS

	To the Reader	ix
I	In the Beginning	1
II	The Years of Discovery	3
III	Under the Spanish Flag	21
IV	The English Come to Stay	29
V	The Growing Years of Freedom	55
VI	In The Land of Cotton	66
VII	The Dark Years of War	79
VIII	The Aftermath	113
IX	A New Beginning	135
	Bibliography	139
	Acknowledgements	141

List of Illustrations

"Published as the Act directs by J.F.W.
DesBarres, Esq., August 10th, 1777."   *frontis.*

                                                 *facing
                                                  page*

The Harbour of Port Royal   10

DeBry Engravings of LeMoyne's Map   11

Typical Pines of Hilton Head   18

Section of Ancient Dugout Excavated by Accident   19

Chalices Dated 1834; Used in Episcopal Zion
    Chapel of Ease   42

Thomas Henry Barksdale   43

Ferry *Pocahontas* Used From 1953 to 1956   43

Baynard Family Mausoleum, Zion Chapel
    Cemetery   50

Cast Iron Caskets Used by Plantation Owners   51

Illustration from *The Soldier In Our Civil War*   74

U.S. Tax Commission Map of City of Hilton
    Head and the Fort, April, 1864   75

Landing of United States Troops at Fort Walker
    After the Bombardment   82

Nursery at Elliott's Plantation   83

Illustrations from *Harper's Weekly*   83

(*List of Illustrations, cont.*)

	facing page
Hilton Head Island Before 1861	106
Map of Hilton Head Showing Its Topography	107
Old Bottle Found at Site of Fort Walker	107
1898 Dynamite Gun Emplacement	114
Drayton's "Fish Haul"	115
Group Being Addressed by Will Clyde	115
Will Clyde and Party	122
One-room Island School, 1955	123
Prehistoric Tooth Found on the Island (*and*) Melted Pennies Found in Ashes of Post Office Fire, 1923	123
Hilton Head Signal Station	130
Earth Defenses at Fort Sherman	131
Post Office (1952) Showing a "Marsh Tacky" and its Colt	131

To The Reader

You who make the James F. Byrnes Crossing to discover Hilton Head and its neighbor islands join a long list of discoverers whose explorations reach far back into the unknown past. Long before there were bridges to cross or even people to build them, the great beasts of pre-history roamed this land. How many of those huge, ungainly beasts were here, or when, we do not fully know, but island roadbuilders have found a giant-sized fossil tooth that could have ached in some mastodon's head thousands of years ago.

Other fossil remains of beasts no longer seen on land or sea may still lie buried in our island soil: the bones of giant sloths, the long, curving ivory tusks of hairy elephants, the fantastically enormous teeth of ancient sharks whose jaws were eight or nine feet wide. They could still be here, for the beasts were here—and the land was here—before history began.

Much of the island's history is told in the following pages, but the tale cannot be complete. History is like an old jigsaw puzzle that has been put away carelessly. When it is finally brought out again, some of the pieces are broken or blank or missing altogether. It may be your luck to find some of the missing pieces and so have a part in re-telling this sea island chronicle. Good hunting!

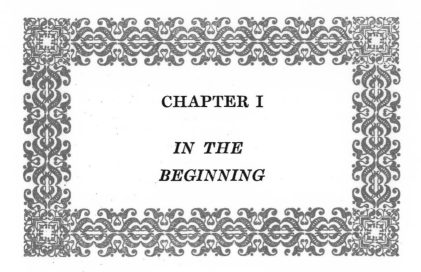

CHAPTER I

IN THE
BEGINNING

THE LAND was here before history began. Covered by the waters of the ancient ocean, it lay dark and life-giving, awaiting its place in the sun. At last, in some tempestuous upheaval, the land rose from the sea and foam-flecked waves washed its brown shoreline. Huge beasts with evil-toothed jaws and ungainly bodies came to roam its marshlands. The rains fell upon the land and the rivers flowed down to it from the inland hills, and at length the sea tides swept their path between it and the farther shore, and the island was separate, a place apart.

Shaped not unlike the tooth from the jaws of those giant, pre-historic beasts, the island lay lengthwise to the shore. Its broad headland faced the northeastern sea and sky, and on either side its banks sloped down with sculptured bay and inlet to the jagged, root-end, southern tip.

The creatures of the sea swam round about it, from great whales and sharks to tiny shellfish. Long-nosed dolphins surfaced nearby, arched lithe gray bodies and dived back down beneath the waves. Ashore there were the animals of woodland and meadow, both large and small, timid and rapacious, and there were also the birds of field, forest, marshland and seaside.

People came. Copper-skinned people who came to hunt for food and stayed on the island and called it home. There were copper-skinned people on the island three thousand years—perhaps four thousand—before a white man ever looked upon it or touched foot to island soil. But it was the white man who first put the island in written history. The earliest copper-skinned islanders left no written records, and only buried fragments of the things they used and bones they gnawed prove their presence. We cannot even be sure if they had a name for themselves or their island home, for only written records can keep names alive when the people who remember them are gone. So it is that the earliest name we can find for our island belongs to the time of the first white explorers. "What is this place and what do you call yourselves?" the white men asked the islanders. But having asked the question, these bold white adventurers paid little heed to the answer. They were looking for India, and whether they had found it or not, they called the copper-skinned people Indians, and so Indians they have always been in written history.

This much we do know about the old names: The "Indians" who were living on this island when the first Europeans came were most probably named for the great chief Maccou, also spelled Maccoa in the early records. Spelling being a very uncertain thing in those days, the tribal name was also written Escamacu, Eesquamaquu, Uscamacu, Camacu, and several other ways, according to the ear and pen of the recorder. These Escamacu (to use the commonest spelling) owed allegiance to the larger tribal group called Oristas, also spelled Audusta, Usta, Edistow and other ways. The Escamacu and Orista people belonged to the Cusabo confederacy of tribes. These Cusabo people are described in the book, *Early Creek Indians and Their Neighbors*, by John R. Swanton, outstanding authority on Indian ways, and their story is also told in *Red Carolinians* by Chapman J. Milling. Many Indian relics have already been found on the island—arrowheads, bits of pottery, shell tools, ornaments. Some of the most ancient are buried in doughnut-shaped mounds, while others are washed in along the shore or spaded up in roadways or gardens. Many more arrowheads and fragments must still lie buried in island soil, but there are no longer any Escamacu people nor any full-blooded Cusabo Indians here or elsewhere.

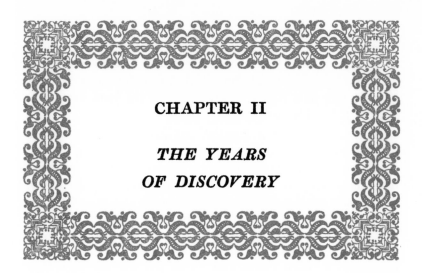

CHAPTER II

THE YEARS
OF DISCOVERY

I T IS just barely possible that the first European to see our island was the Italian, Amerigo Vespucci, for whom America was named. Vespucci might have glimpsed it from the deck of his sailing ship in 1497, although the true course of his voyages has never been determined and many historians do not believe he came this far north. Perhaps the Englishman Sebastian Cabot also saw this island in that same year. Cabot claimed to have sailed south along the coast from Newfoundland to 29° north latitude, and the faulty calculations of those days might have given him honest reason to think so. However, he was at sea such a short time that so long a voyage hardly seems possible. But at least it is generally granted that his father, John Cabot, a Venetian exploring for England, had already discovered part of this continent, landing near Newfoundland. With the usual broad sea-to-sea, claim-it-all-explore-it-later policy of those days, Cabot had boldly declared the whole continent to be English soil forever to its farthest limits.

Fifteen years later Juan Ponce de León made the same sort of far-reaching claim for Spain, although Ponce made his discovery at the continent's southern tip. Kneeling on the sandy shore of the southern peninsula, he named the new land "Tierra Florida," because he had discovered it at Eastertide, which in Spanish is called "La Pascua Florida." To him and to all Spaniards thereafter, this land of Florida was now theirs as far north as the land extended, even if it be clear to the Polar Seas.

Neither Spanish nor English navigators had yet landed on our sea island, so far as we know, nor had the roving Portuguese or Italians, although someone besides Vespucci may have seen it. The Italian Verrazno, among others, made maps of this coastline, but their hit-and-miss methods of map-making do not prove discovery. Coasting close to shore one day and blown out of sight of land the next, those early explorers filled in their maps with a wiggly line here, a curve there, and often did not see half they charted.

Putting aside all these "might-have-been" discoveries we turn to the hundreds of written letters and documents filed in the Spanish "Archivos de las Indias"—Archives of the Indies—and find the first real proof of discovery. With this written proof before us, we can say surely that the first white men to set foot on our island, the first to give it a name, were Spaniards. Their story has been re-told in English by Woodbury Lowery in his two-volume history, *Spanish Settlements in the United States*, in Justin Winsor's *Narrative and Critical History of America* and in many other books. The story began in the year 1520 with a dream in the heart of a bold Spaniard named Lucas Vásquez de Ayllón.

Now Lucas Vásquez de Ayllón was an official of some importance in the Spanish colony at Santa Domingo. He had a lovely wife, a fine young son, wealth, power. But he yearned above all else to have the honor of discovering new lands. It was a yearning that stirred many a Spanish heart in those venturesome days, and De Ayllón had no difficulty in finding captain and crew to undertake the voyage as soon as he received royal permission for exploration. The license was granted early in 1521 and De Ayllón persuaded his friend Diego Caballero to share the cost of the voyage. As nearly as we can find out, neither De Ayllón nor Caballero was able to sail on the caravel they fitted for the venture. At the last moment both were kept at home by their official duties, and there they stood on the quay at La Plata harbor waving farewell as the small vessel with its broad bows and high narrow poop weighed anchor and headed out to sea.

"Que vaya con Diós!" they surely called after her. "Que vaya bien! Buen viaje!" All their wishes were with her, all their hopes for glory.

The caravel's captain was one Francisco Gordillo, and whether he lived up to the meaning of his last name— "little fat one"—is not known. The pilot was Alonzo Fernandez Sotil. Without his skill the little vessel would surely have encountered even more difficulties than were already allotted to it.

Now it came about that shortly after leaving port they came in sight of another caravel captained by Pedro de Quexos, a man well known to Sotil. The two ships exchanged salutes and dropped anchors, and presently De Quexos boarded the other vessel for a visit. Perhaps he did not confide to Gordillo that he was really searching for Carib Indians to sell as slaves in the gold mines of Santo Domingo. The kidnapping of Indians for slaves was not given royal approval at that time so it is unlikely that De Quexos tattled of the matter. Probably he simply mentioned that one of his sponsors was Juan Oriz de Matienzo, an official in Santo Domingo well known to De Ayllón and of good standing. However, De Quexos did offer to join Gordillo on his voyage of exploration. After all, this bold Pedro must have reasoned to himself, he had not found any slaves as yet, so why not go exploring? Besides, two ships were infinitely better than one on strange seas. As to the latter theory, Gordillo was in quick agreement. Side by side, their white lateen sails ruffling to the breeze, the two caravels set out along the unknown coast. Sometimes they could see plainly the brown shoreline with its green fringe of islands, but when there was only gray-blue ocean stretching in unending waves from dawn horizon to sunset sky, then even those bold hearts must have quickened in fear and wonder that the world could be so wide.

On a bright June day they reckoned themselves at about

37° north latitude and well beyond the territory granted to Ponce de León's personal rule, although still considered part of Florida. Sighting a good harbor at the mouth of a river, Gordillo quickly assembled a landing party and with a prayer of Thanksgiving named the river San Juan (Saint John). They had no sooner slashed tree trunks with a cross as sign of His Catholic Majesty, King Charles of Spain, than brown-skinned natives appeared. These "Indios" seemed friendly enough and full of curiosity about the white-skinned, bearded strangers who came riding into harbor on wooden sea monsters with white wings.

Now De Ayllón had told Gordillo to treat any Indians he found with all fairness, since the King himself so wished it and would not grant license for colonization without this rule. Such a license with its usual titles of adelantado and gobernador was what De Ayllón wanted, and so he had given his captain strict orders. But De Quexos, who had started out as a slave runner in the first place, owed his sponsor no such promise and he began to lay schemes. He let Gordillo make friends with the Indians, but there must have been a greedy glint in his eyes the while. They had landed, so they understood the Indians to say, in the land of Chicora. Just to the south was the land of Orista and the two provinces were friendly one with another. Gordillo signed that he was a friend also and invited some fifty or more Indians aboardship for a feast.

This was the very chance De Quexos was waiting for. Just how he persuaded Gordillo to join him in his evil plan—or whether Gordillo was tricked into it—the records do not say. But the Archivos de las Indias in Sevilla, Spain, do reveal that while the Indian guests were still celebrating below-deck, the Spaniards weighed treacherous anchor and put out to sea in a good stiff breeze. With the first lurch to seaward the guests became guests no longer, but captives bound for the slave markets of Hispaniola.

In a moment the Indians discovered their betrayal and came swarming to the deck ready to leap overboard and swim to shore. The Spaniards drew their swords. No pretense of friendship now. The rough sailors quickly over-

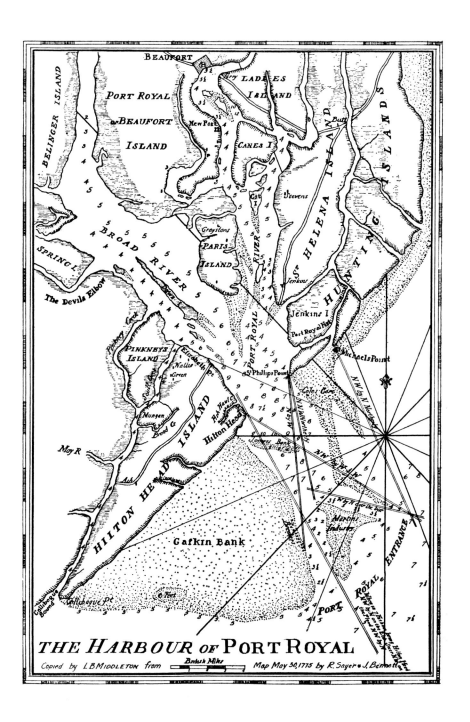

THE *HARBOUR* OF PORT ROYAL

Copied by LB MIDDLETON from — British Miles — Map May 30,1775 by R. Sayer & J. Bennett

DeBry Engravings of LeMoyne's Maps

powered their captives and locked them in the hold with greedy glee. Slaves fetched good prices in Santo Domingo and the Spaniards could almost hear the coins jingling in their pouches.

But even as they counted the promised gold it was snatched away from them. The sky blackened and the stiff breeze swept to gale force. All alone in the storm-driven sea the two caravels pitched and tossed. Wild water washed over the broad bows, over the high and narrow poop. One of the vessels sank. Perhaps Gordillo sank with it, for his name vanished from the records of exploration. Many of the captives drowned also. De Quexos rescued what men he could, white-skinned or brown, and rode out the storm.

When at last the sea quieted and the storm clouds cleared away De Quexos saw before him a bold, bluff headland topped with the tall green spires of pine trees. Sailing closer he saw it was the entrance to a wide harbor, and never had any harbor or any land looked so fair. The date, according to ship's calendar, was August the eighteenth, the feast day of Santa Elena (Saint Helena, mother of Emperor Constantine of Greece). With true Catholic fervor De Quexos named the land for the saint on whose day it had been revealed to him and stepping ashore for a brief moment, claimed it for Spain, for Holy Catholic Church and for De Ayllón the licensed explorer. Having done so, he ascertained that he was in the latitude of 32 degrees north and set quick sail for home port.

Calculations of the exact latitude of the land of Santa Elena would vary in the many records in the Archives of the Indies, but we can be fairly certain that the bold bluff headland De Quexos sighted on August 18, 1521, was the very promontory we now call Hilton Head. The name of Santa Elena was not for the headland alone, but for the whole territory, for as one document in the Archives sums up the voyage, De Ayllòn reported that his captains had "disembarked various times in different places, and in particular in the provinces of Chicora and Orista to which *district* was given the name Santa Elena, because it was discovered on her day." The writer of this statement was

Antonio de Arredondo, who followed an earlier report by Andrés Gonzales Barcia, and his exact words in Spanish are:

"Desembarcando varias veces en distintos parages, y en particular en las provincias de Chicora y Orista, a cuya jurisdicion puso por nombre 'Santa Elena', por haverla descubierto en su dia."

Arredondo's report was called *Demostration Historiografica Del Derecho De Espana A Nueva Georgia* and has been translated into English by Professor Herbert E. Bolton of the University of California, who added other information from his own extensive research.

Apparently De Quexos did not realize on this first voyage that he had discovered an island, for he does not refer to the "isla" of Santa Elena but mentions the "punta" or "cabo"—headland or cape. However, the point or cape of Santa Elena is truly Hilton Head according to the decision of two officials of the United States Coast and Geodetic Survey, Mr. Herbert C. Graves and Mr. O. H. Tittman, who made a careful study of the many charts and records available. One of those records is the "Relación de la Costa de Florida" by Juan de Herrera, manuscript number 4541 in the National Library in Madrid, translated in Woodbury Lowery's history of the Spanish settlements:

". . . from Santa Elena to the northeast is the point of Santa Elena itself, and it is an island itself, for the sea washes between it and the land . . . To the northeast of the cape of Santa Elena is a very good river . . . and these shoals extend fully three leagues from the land into the sea . . . It has three or four entrances . . . In the midst of the bay you will find within it an island in the middle of the river which is shaped like a galley . . . To the northeast of the cape of Santa Elena is another river which has a good bar, where is the first Indian village."

The island shaped like a galley is probably the present Parris Island, and the island with the first Indian village is probably the island now called Saint Helena. But the present St. Helena was surely not the land first sighted by De Quexos, for it is plainly too far within the channel. With the Coast and Geodetic Survey and the Archives of the Spanish Indies to back us up, we can say again that our island was discovered by Pedro de Quexos and his crew of Spanish explorers on August 18, 1521. One of the earliest maps to show the cape of Santa Elena is that drawn by Diego Ribero, Spanish royal cosmographer, in 1529. Although Ribero marks his "c de Sta. Elena" opposite a cape, not an island, the contour is enough like our present Hilton Head to remove any reasonable doubt. Records of further exploration make identification even surer.

Meanwhile De Quexos reached home port with only a few sickly starvelings instead of the fifty husky slaves he had hoped to sell at high prices in Hispaniola market, for most of the Indians had chosen to starve rather than accept food from their hated captors. With a Spaniard's ready ease in taking fortune where he finds it, De Quexos turned to De Ayllón and swore that he too, yearned for further exploration and would serve his sponsor well. De Ayllón hired him on the spot. But first he had to settle at court the the matter of the kidnapped Indians. Presiding over the court was Diego Columbus, son of the famous admiral, and he ruled that the Indians must be returned to their homeland as soon as possible. De Ayllón agreed. He had no choice. Although Spaniards in America had already enslaved thousands of Indios and would enslave thousands more before their rule was ended, the official attitude of the moment was against slavery and any man who wanted a favor from the king had to take the king's attitude as his own.. So De Ayllón accepted Diego Columbus' rule with good grace, asking only that he first be allowed time to go to Spain and request in person a royal license for actual colonization. So it was arranged, and De Ayllón took with him to Spain as his personal servant one of the more biddable Indians, now a baptized Christian re-named Francisco Chicorana, or Francisco of Chicora.

This Francisco had a lively imagination and his tales of the marvelous Santa Elena kept Spanish courtiers in Madrid listening agog for many a day. It was, he said, a land of self-made giants created by softening and stretching the bones during childhood. There were also people with tails, tails as hard as bone, a full cubit in length, so that their chairs must needs have openings in the seat for the tail to pass through, or else holes must be dug in the earth before they could sit in comfort. Deer were tame as household pets and gave milk like cows. Pearls were as abundant as pebbles.

"And jewels?" asked the eager courtiers.

Francisco nodded, his inventive genius limited only by Spanish credulity, for who was there in this land to gainsay him? Charter member of any Tall Tales League or New World Liars Club, he spun the yarns as long as anyone would listen. No wonder that it was June 12, 1523, before De Ayllòn was finally granted his license and allowed to leave. He was now "Licenciado"—licensed colonizer—De Ayllón with the sole right to settle Chicora, Orista and seventeen other provinces Francisco had glibly reeled off as belonging in Santa Elena.

Gathering men and provisions for a new colony was no small task and it was after New Year's Day in 1525 before De Ayllón's two caravels were ready to set sail. Much to his dismay the conscientious Licenciado was again kept from sailing with his ships by the heavy responsibilities of his office as auditor. With a sigh of resignation he gave Pedro de Quexos full charge and stayed at home to serve his king with pen and record book instead of conqueror's sword. It was, perhaps, the role for which he was better fitted. While the man's keen intellect and upright character were generally praised, he was not rated highly as a soldier, "never having donned armor or borne a sword to earn a soldier's pay," as his friend the Spanish historian Gonzales Fernandez Oviedo y Valdez put it.

So, without their sponsor's presence—except in spirit—the two caravels explored the coast for a distance of some two hundred fifty leagues, roughly about six hundred miles. De Quexos did not attempt to found a settlement, leaving that honor for De Ayllón himself but he did take possession of all he saw in the name of King Charles and erected stone pillars or slashed Christian crosses on tree trunks to support the claim. His ships were back in the harbor of Santo Domingo by the first of July. As trophies De Quexos brought home a little gold and silver and a few pearls. He also had with him several Indians from the various tribes he had encountered, and he assured De Ayllón that these were not kidnapped slaves but men who had come willingly to see the white man's world and learn his speech. They would be of invaluable help as interpreters when De Ayllón would take his place at Indian council fires. No doubt an Indian from the island tribe of the chief Maccou was among them, although no name has come down to us.

Meanwhile another Spaniard, Esteban Gomez by name, must have sighted Santa Elena, for in the year 1525 his lone caravel cruised the entire Atlantic coastline from the English Newfoundland—which he called "Tierra de Baccalaos," land of the codfish—to "Tierra Florida." Gomez was in search of that will-o-the-wisp dream, the Northwest Passage to the Orient, and it was his chart which served as guide for the mapmaker Diego Ribero.

Of course Gomez did not find the non-existent passage and while he was returning home in despair, Lucas Vásquez de Ayllón was making joyful preparation to start out on his own long-delayed voyage. In the middle of July, 1526, he sailed from the port of La Plata in Hispaniola with a fleet of six good-sized vessels and a small tender. Aboard ship were six hundred men and women. Some accounts say he had only three ships and five hundred colonists, but all agree that among the group were several doctors, an apothecary, a number of Negro slaves and three Dominican friars. Thus with one hand did Spain bring slavery and Christ's cross to Santa Elena and the two would remain in the land long after the black-haired Spaniards had withdrawn. De Ayllón had also bethought him to bring one hundred (some say eighty-nine) good horses, and these too—or at least their descendants—would outlast Spanish rule, and there is still said to be the blood of Spanish steeds in Hilton Head marsh ponies.

But De Ayllón guessed nothing of the future and the

shortness of life span still left to him in these days and sailed out of Hispaniola harbor with good heart. Not finding the cape of Santa Elena to his liking, for some strange reason, he sailed on after only a short stay. Perhaps he was lured on by the hope of seeing Francisco Chicorana's giants and people with tails. At any event, he went to a river somewhat beyond 33° north latitude, according to his reckoning, which he named he River Jordan. He may have taken the name from the Bible, but a report persists that he named it for his pilot, although such a name so completely un-Spanish has not been found listed for any crew member. The River Jordan is usually identified as the River Santee, but it could have been elsewhere. There Tall Tale Francisco ran away never to be seen again.

There also one of Ayllon's ships was wrecked and the colonists doggedly set about building another, an open boat called in Spanish a "gavarra" with a single mast and provided with oars to use when the wind failed. Building even such a small boat was no easy task and the accomplishment proves how staunch and resourceful De Ayllòn's group really was. While some of the men worked and hammered and sawed or caulked new seams wih the gray moss that hung on forest trees, others looked about for a permanent homesite. We will probably never know just which spot they chose for this first white settlement within the boundaries of what is now the United States. Some historians think they sailed south, some north of 33° and the River Jordan. We do know that they named the town San Miguel (St. Michael) and usually added the Indian name for the region and spoke of the settlement as "San Miguel de Gualdape." Gualdape, like most Indian words translated to Spanish and other tongues was probably twisted in the process. Many historians think it meant the Indian province called Guale, lying just south of the province of Orista with the boundary line near the punta de Santa Elena. But the name Guale was also used for an inland town not far from Port Royal. Later it was used for the sea island of St. Catherine. Still later it was used to mean the colony of Georgia, and the English colonists wrote the name "Wallie" in imitation of the Spanish pronunciation. So even if we were sure that San Miguel de Gualdape was really in Guale, we still would not be sure of its exact location.

Wherever it was, the new colony suffered bitter hardship in that winter of 1526. Many of the Spaniards sickened and died, Ayllòn among them. His nephew Juan Ramirez succeeded as leader, but he did not have the licenciado's authority and there were hot quarrels and jealousy. The Negro slaves revolted. When at last only one hundred and fifty hungry wretches were left of the five or six hundred souls who had set out, San Miguel was abandoned forever and the pitiful survivors sailed home to the Indies in despair. They tried to take Ayllón's body with them, but the ship carrying it was lost at sea.

The report of their misadventures did not exactly stir up enthusiasm for a new attempt. Ayllòn's son did apply for a license to carry on his father's claim to the "Tierra de Ayllón" or "Tierra del licenciado Ayllón" as the map makers now labeled it, but he died before a license was granted.

Some years later the governor of Mexico sent Tristan de Luna y Arellano to occupy Santa Elena, but De Luna's ships were wrecked near Pensacola and before he could reorganize his fleet, the governor sent Angel de Villafañe to supersede him. A good share of De Luna's crew followed the new leader, who had orders to be on the lookout for castaways from a Spanish fleet captained by Farfan, shipwrecked near Santa Elena that December. Villafañe was also supposed to look over the land and report on its possibilities as a settlement.

On the 27th of May, 1561, Villafañe arrived in Santa Elena, or so he claimed, although his pilot Gonzalo Gayon declared that they were in 33° north latitude. Villafañe found neither inhabitants nor a likely harbor and after some further exploration returned to Hispaniola with an unfavorable report. Felipe II was now King of Spain and it was his opinion that further colonization of Santa Elena was pointless. Who would be interested in a little green land of woods and marshes when there was all that gold and silver in Mexico and Peru?

So the Indians of Santa Elena were left alone for a time
to plant their fields of maize, to build their houses of logs
thatched with palmetto leaves, play their beloved game of
throwing a spear at a rolling ball, and drink their black brew
of yaupon (cassina) leaves. They were still there living in
peace and plenty, when another white-sailed ship from still
another land across the sea came nosing into the harbor in
1562.

The ship was French.   Its captain was the energetic,
bushy-bearded Jean Ribaut. The chief sponsor behind the
expedition was the nobleman Gaspard, comte de Coligny,
seigneur de Chatillon-sur-Loing, admiral of France, and it
was rumored that the Queen Mother herself, the ever-
scheming Catherine de Medici, had also contributed to it.
The colonists aboard the vessel were French Huguenots
seeking refuge from anti-Protestant persecution in Catholic
France. There is some evidence to prove that the sponsors,
at least—if not the colonists themselves—hoped to make
their fortune robbing Spanish treasure ships homeward
bound with their booty of Inca and Aztec gold.

Now the Spaniards had done everything within their
power to keep their sea charts out of alien hands and so
safeguard the treasures of the Indies for themselves. But
French, English and Portuguese captains dangled tempting
bribes before the eyes of any Spanish pilot who had sailed
the Bahama Channel and eventually some of them weak-
ened and betrayed the treasure routes. Then, too, some
enterprising French or Portuguese pilots had managed to
pass themselves off as true Spaniards and so get a berth
on some Spanish caravel, galleon or brigantine bound for
those enchanted shores. Somehow this Jean Ribaut had got
hold of a Portuguese pilot who knew the Florida coast and
from him or from some pilfered map, Ribaut had learned
the name and location of Santa Elena. He wasn't just cruis-
ing about when he sighted our bluff headland. He knew
where he was going. With him as second in command was
René Laudonnière and although neirther attempted to draw
a map of Santa Elena they did write enthusiastic descrip-
tions of the new land and both accounts would be published

in both English and French when the adventurers finally returned home.

Here in the new world they sailed past the island guarding the harbor and exclaimed with delight at the broadness of the waterway before them, ample enough to shelter the largest ships France could boast. Certainly there was room for their small fleet consisting of two Dutch three-masted vessels and one large sloop. They promptly christened the harbor "Port Royale . . . because of the largenesse and fairnesse thereof" and this name would endure on maps and charts of all languages forever after, pronounced as easily in Spanish or English as in French itself. Like the Spanish title of Santa Elena this new name of Port Royale was intended to include the whole area, although in time it would be used for one island, one river, one town.

Ribaut did not set up camp on our sea island where any passing Spanish ship might have sighted him, but went on a good three leagues within the channel (or at least most historians think so) to the island now called Parris—for the Englishman Alexander Parris who later bought it, not for the French capital. Ribaut had already set up at least one stone pillar engraved with the royal arms of France somewhere along the Florida coast and now he erected another near the new town site. He named the town "Charlesfort" in honor of his twelve-year-old king, Charles the Ninth, and it was the first Protestant settlement—and the second white settlement—in what is now the United States. As soon as the site was established, he assigned to Laudonniére the task of finding another attractive place where a pillar claiming French possession might be erected. Laudonniére's journal, translated into English by his contemporary Richard Hakluyt, records it thus:

"This done, we imbarked ourselves and sayled three leagues toward the West, where wee discovered a little river up which wee sayled so long that in the end wee found it returned into the great current and in the return to make a little Island separated from the firme land where we went ashore; and by commandment of the Capitaine, because it was exceeding faire and pleasant, there wee planted a Pillar upon a hillock open round about to the view, and invironed with a lake halfe a fathom deepe of very good and sweet water."

Ribaut and Laudonnière now made friends with the Indians and explored all the island roundabout, quite confident that they were seeing "more in six weeks than the Spaniards had done in two years," as Laudonnière wrote in his journal. Perhaps they did, for here and there on the coast Indian legend has come down the years that the first white man to be seen had—like Ribaut—a full beard of reddish-gold hue. However much or little Ribaut saw, he was surely enthusiastic. "The aboundance of fish as is increadable," he noted in Hakluyt's translation. "Havens and rivers and islands of such frutefulnesse as cannot with tongue be expressed."

It was too fair a land to leave with only a stone pillar as proof of French possession, and so Ribaut asked for volunteers to stay behind at Charlesfort while he returned for the families and provisions. More voluntered than were needed and Ribaut chose twenty-eight—some reports say only twenty-five, others thirty or thirty-four—and then he and Laudonnière and the others returned to France. The little group of brand-new residents of a brand-new world watched the white sails disappear and turned to look at each other in half-frightened awe. As far as they knew they were the only white men between the Spanish Indies and the cold land of the codfish. Then with a cheerful French shrug of acceptance they settled down to make the best of what they had. They had ammunition and guns and some small stock of provisions. The Indians had willingly brought gifts of corn, beans, several kinds of squashes and dried berries. There were fish in the sea and deer in the forest. And of course Ribaut would be back in six months.

Six months passed—and more—and Ribaut did not come. The friendly Indians near Charlesfort were running out of food, and so the Frenchmen borrowed a dugout canoe and traveled to another Indian village called Ouade (probably the same town the Spanish spelled *Guale*) to beg of their stores. Food was cheerfully given, for such was the

Indian custom when their own people were in need and they made no exception of the white-skinned strangers. But even these added supplies did not last forever and the French were soon hungry again. Constantly expecting Ribaut's return, they did not even try to plant crops of their own. To add to their troubles, their storehouse burned to the ground and everything they owned burned with it, except the clothes on their backs. The Indians promptly helped them rebuild their house, but there was no way of replacing the food and clothing.

Quarrels rise easily on empty stomachs. The wooden walls of Charlesfort echoed back angry oaths and threats and hothead quarreling. The captain appointed by Ribaut, Albert de la Pierria, seemed unable to keep the peace or his own temper. He hanged one man for small offense and exiled another named Lachére to a neighboring island. Finally the men revolted, slew Pierria and elected Nicholas Barré in his stead.

Rumor spread that six of the men had met a band of strange Indians somewhere in the woods and taken from them four hundred thousand ducats of Spanish gold. The tale was credible enough, for Spanish treasure ships were frequently wrecked along the Florida coast. The others clamored for their share of the booty, but apparently the gold was never dug up from its hiding place. It may still lie buried in Port Royale Land, perhaps on our own island.

Barré decided that staying longer was impossible. Building an ocean-going vessel seemed impossible, also, but like the Spaniards before them, these hardy French adventurers managed to do it. Although the French had never heard of the *gavarra* built by De Ayllón's crew, their own boat looked very much like it, with one mast and a set of oars. The sail they made from their own shirts, piecing and patching as best they could.

One lad, seventeen-year-old Guillaume Rouffi, took one look at this unseaworthy concoction and bethought him how little these landlubber soldiers knew of navigating on the wide ocean. No more than he knew, certainly, and that was naught. Rouffi decided to stay with the friendly Indians, and they accepted him as one of them and dressed him as they dressed, in deerskin and feathers.

Rouffi's fear of the voyage was justified. The little boat was becalmed in mid-ocean. The voyagers turned cannibal and ate Lachère—whom they had rescued from his exile island for this sorry fate—and perhaps ate another man also. Finally an English ship rescued them, and so some of the poor wretches did reach home. There they discovered that Ribaut had not willfully neglected them. He had reached his home town of Dieppe in time to join the Huguenot army battling there for religious freedom, and when Dieppe fell he had fled to England. There he had tried to match wits with Queen Elizabeth, pretending to accept a bribe from her and give her the French colony at Charlesfort in return for Protestant English help against the Spanish dons. When the English ships were ready to sail, Ribaut tried to slip away, but he was caught and thrown into prison.

Back in France the Admiral de Coligny managed to get together another group of Huguenot colonists, and with René Laudonnière in command, the new expedition made ready. Remembering that there were more wonders in the new world than could "with tongue be expressed," Laudonnière enrolled an artist among the others, a very skillful engraver and painter named Jacques LeMoyne de Margues. All the way across the ocean LeMoyne listened to the tales of Charlesfort told by Laudonnière and others who had been there, and before long he felt he knew the place well enough to draw pictures of it. He showed his sketches to the others and they crowded around him eagerly. There was the island shaped like a galley. There was bearded Jean Ribaut himself stepping from his ship to the island where Charlesfort had been built amid green-branched cedar trees. There were the Indians they had seen roasting a lynx whelp over a fire. There was the island at the harbor mouth where they had found the biggest deer, and the smaller island where they had erected the pillar. There were the Indians at Ouade. They laughed and clapped LeMoyne on the back and praised him. Who would guess he had never been there when he drew everything so clearly? they said.

But LeMoyne was not quite so clear as we would wish. Moreover, all but one of his original paintings were lost, and we have only engraved copies to study. These engravings were made by Theodore DeBry, a Huguenot refugee from Flanders who escaped to England and later met LeMoyne there. LeMoyne, like many another French Protestant, eventually settled down to live in England. He married an English girl, anglicized his name to James Margues and worked in the household of Sir Walter Raleigh. On the side he did some art work for Richard Hakluyt, the editor who translated Ribaut's and Laudonniére's journals. However, he refused to let anyone publish his own sketches of the new world, either those of Charlesfort and Port Royale or those of the second French settlement that Laudonniére had named Fort Caroline. Probably he was always hopeful of getting back to his old trade of engraver and bookseller and so be able to publish his own work. He died, however, with his pictures unpublished, and his widow sold them to DeBry who promptly put out three editions in French, English and German all at the same time. Probably as a thrifty scheme for making one set of engravings serve for all three editions, DeBry labeled LeMoyne's maps and drawings with Latin names. (See maps facing page 11).

The name of Charlesfort was not translated into Latin, but Fort Caroline became *Arx Carolina*. Santa Elena was marked *S. Helenae*, and Port Royale, *Portus Regalis*. Ribaut is seen stepping from his boat to *Cedrorum Insulam* (Island of the Cedars), while the place where the pillar stands—and where Hilton Head Island should be—is marked *Liburni*. This Latin word *Liburni* is usually translated as Liburnia or Libourne, an old name for the country now called Croatia, but no explanation for its use is given. Perhaps we should allow for a slip of the engraving pen— or poor Latin—and grant that DeBry meant to write *Liburna*, the Latin word for a small vessel of war, a schooner or brigantine. Such a name would be very plausible, since old accounts frequently mention an island shaped like a small sailing vessel or galley lying in Port Royal Harbor.

The name Liburni does not seem to stand for the whole of Hilton Head Island but only the high-tide island at the northwestern tip, now known as Bobb's Island. Some historians believe that Bobb is only the changeling form of Ribaut, evolved after years of twisting and turning by many tongues. So it may be, for a French name mispronounced for years by Indians and Spaniards and Englishmen and Gullah Negroes could be changed into almost anything. Whether Bobb's Island is really Ribaut's Island and whether a stone pillar engraved with the arms of France once stood there will probably never be known. We have only LeMoyne's maps to go by, and LeMoyne himself was never here.

Later French maps drop the name Liburni and usually call Hilton Head Island, *Ile de la Riviere Grande*—island of the broad (or large) river. Ribaut had given French names to all the rivers and some islands and capes from Florida northward, but mapmakers did not always agree as to which places were which. When Nicolas Bellin drew his map in 1744 he frankly admitted this uncertainty by labelling *"Ici devoit être le cap Ste. Hélène," "Ici devoit être Cap Fancois."* Here they *should be*, or *must be*—not here they are!

However wrong or right these early maps and pictures are, they give us the only glimpse we can get of what the first explorers thought they saw in the land of the Escamacu, the land of Spanish Santa Elena and French Port Royale, one day to be our own Hilton Head.

CHAPTER III

UNDER THE
SPANISH FLAG

I T DID not take the Spanish long to hear of the French colony of Charlesfort at Santa Elena and to realize that Felipe II had made a mistake in deciding that no one would want to settle there. Could they tolerate a foreign settlement so near the route of the Spanish treasure fleets? Risk French capture of the millions of dollars of gold and silver shipped yearly from the Indies? By their Spanish beards, NO! The French must be wiped out!

So don Hernando Manrique de Rojas set out for Santa Elena in the spring of 1564, determined to oust every Frenchman from Spanish domain. Little did he guess that all but one of those hated French Protestants had already departed and that a new colony was heading for a post even closer to the route of the treasure fleets. He had heard of the French stone pillars erected along the Florida coast and stopped several times to search for them, but not one could he find. When he finally reached Santa Elena, he found it deserted, but the Indians told him of the French lad living in their town of Usta, possibly the place the Spanish called Orista. At any rate, it was not far off and Manrique sent an Indian runner with a wooden cross to show the French lad that Christians were waiting to see him. When Guillaume Rouffi appeared, Manrique promptly took him prisoner with a zeal that might have been patriotic but was certainly not Christian. With Spanish muskets and sword points to persuade him, Rouffi led his captors to the place where Laudonniére had erected the stone pillar. Manrique triumphantly ordered it torn out and put aboard ship, so that he could carry it back to Spain as visible proof of mission accomplished. Although the record of its arrival in Spain was duly entered in the Archives, the report was not made public, and so the French pillar has been hunted for high and low all over the sea islands. If there were two pillars erected here, as Laudonnière's journal seems to indicate, one of them might still be awaiting discovery, although a pillar on tiny Bobb's Island would surely have been swallowed by the stormy waves long since.

Not even dreaming of a second pillar, Manrique sailed for home, keeping the French lad with him. Translated to the Spanish form of Guillermo Rufin, the boy's name appeared on more than one document in the Archives of the Indies and he apparently served the Spaniards from then on. If he must be dubbed traitor, let it be remembered that he was only a boy and had small chance to choose otherwise. His own homeland had already persecuted him for his religion. The Indians had given him over to the Spaniards. Where else could he turn?

Meanwhile Laudonnière had landed on the Florida coast and found the pillar he and Ribaut had put there. The Indians had kept it garlanded with flowers and placed gifts before it as if it were an altar. There in late June the new Fort Caroline was begun, with LeMoyne on hand to sketch every happening in bright colors. Eventually Ribaut joined them, freed from his English imprisonment just in time to be present at the vicious attack on Fort Caroline by Spanish forces under don Pedro Menéndez de Avilés. For of course the Spaniards were even more determined to obliterate this second French intrusion than they had been to wipe out faraway Charlesfort. It is a wonder that any of the Frenchmen escaped, for Menèndez fell to the butchery with good conscience, since these imposters were not only enemies of Spain but Protestant heretics, enemies of the Holy Catholic Church. It was the time of the

Typical Pines of Hilton Head

Kenneth Rogers

Section of Ancient Dugout Excavated by Accident

Orion D. Hack

Spanish Inquisition and heretics were doomed men, friend or foe.

With the French settlement destroyed, Menéndez now built a Spanish fort named San Augústin (St. Augustine). He also had orders to build a fort at Santa Elena, but it was 1566 before he was free to do so. He named the new fort San Felipe (St. Phillip) and one of the many islands in Port Royal harbor still bears this name, although that does not prove that it was the site of the original Spanish fort. More probably San Felipe was on Parris Island, for its nearness to the destroyed French Charlesfort is often mentioned in the Archives. Pedro Menéndez, nephew of Menéndez de Avilés, was named governor, and Esteban de las Alas, vice-governor. Men, women and children, doctors, apothecaries, farmers and priests were in the new colony, and besides claiming the land for Spain their chief duty was to convert the heathen Indians to the Catholic faith.

The first missionary to preach on these coastal islands— if we except the three Dominican friars with Ayllón, who evidently did not tarry here—was a Jesuit, Father Juan Rogel. With him was the lay brother, Francisco de Villareal. They erected large wooden crosses at each Indian village from San Augustin northward and no doubt built one on our island. If the Indian braves would not heed him, Father Juan could always get the children to listen by promising them a treat of corn cakes or other food when the lesson was learned. He tried to teach them the Pater Noster, the Ave Maria, the Credo, the Salve and the Commandments, but the Latin words meant less than nothing to them, and the priest knew he would have to settle down in one place and learn the tribal tongue or else conversion would be meaningless.

Two years later Father Juan Bautista de Segura came to Florida from Spain, with three other Jesuit priests and ten brothers, and of these the lay brother Juan de la Carrera is mentioned as being at Santa Elena with Father Juan Rogel. Then Father Juan went to Havana, hoping to establish a Jesuit college there, but in 1570 he was back again in Santa Elena, no doubt discovering that the children had all but forgotten their "Our Father" and "Hail Mary". The good Father now made his headquarters at the Indian village of Orista, some five leagues distance from San Felipe, and in a scant six months he could teach and preach in the Orista tongue. The Indians of Orista were much more biddable than others he had worked with, Father Juan wrote in the many letters he sent home to Spain. Their manner of living was well-ordered and virtuous; they were kindly, good tempered. Since they were of the same tribal affiliation as our own island Escamacus, his description is worth reading for a glimpse at our island's past:

"Each Indian had but one wife, worked hard at his planting and the children were carefully trained. They were neither cruel nor thievish, and unnatural crimes were entirely unknown. They were great traders, expert in barter, carrying their merchandise far into the interior. The elders met in the council house, where the affairs of the tribe were decided. The Indians were truthful, dwelt peaceably among themselves, and were given to but one vice — they were great gamblers and would stake all that they possessed at a game of chance. During the year they passed but two and a half months at their village, planting their corn in the spring, but when the acorn season arrived they scattered through the forests to gather them, and other wild fruits in their season, and only met together at intervals of two months to celebrate their festivals, now at one locality, now at another. Their provisions were held in common and it was their custom to give away their food without demanding anything in return."

Father Juan attended their feasts and council meetings in the various places, including our island, and never missed an opportunity to exhort the Indians to become Christians and so escape the danger of Hell Fire. Love God and hate the Devil, he told them earnestly, turn your back on the Devil and all his works. But he must have used for the word *devil* the name of some respected god or power of the Indian faith, for suddenly the Indians rose against him with angry faces, turned their backs to him and stalked off. Bewildered, Father Juan called after them but they would not listen. His next letter home said:

"So great was the vexation and hatred which they conceived at my words, that never again would they listen to me; and they said to my countrymen that they were angry and did not believe a thing I said, since I spoke ill of the Devil."

Patiently, earnestly, Father Juan went from one Indian to another, trying to win them back to Christ, but the more he talked, the angrier they became, till Father Juan was sure that he was going to "dar la piel"—lose his skin—an expression that may have meant he expected to be scalped.

But at last his sincerity and soft words won him listeners again, and he was able to go on with his work.

He must have given some time in these years to saving the souls of the Spanish soldiers at San Felipe and to the twenty farmers and their wives who were supposed to raise crops to feed the garrison. On his journeys to and from the fort he saw the virgin forests thick with oak, pine and cypress, the many kinds of trees bearing fruits and nuts, and he noted that the Indians knew how to improve their fruit trees by grafting. Probably he had a tolerant smile when some soldier brought him a queer-looking rosary to bless, a rosary made from the nutgrass or ground-nut roots. Those round nodules, strung like beads along the stem, black without and white within, bone-dry and aromatic, looked too much like rosary beads not to be hailed as such. "Santa Elena beads," the Spaniards called them, and many a soldier and sailor carried them off as one more curious trophy from the New World. The Indians valued them, also, but for a different reason. Ground to powder the roots served as a tonic to tighten the skin after bathing and to strengthen the flesh. As internal medicine they would quieten stomach pains or help in the passage of kidney stones, so the Indians claimed.

Father Juan listened to their beliefs, nodding acceptance, eager to keep their friendship. He was troubled now because there seemed to be so much hatred between the Indians and the settlers at San Felipe. The farmers were so afraid of Indian attack that most of them did not go out to the fields to tend their crops, and as a result the storehouses were nearly empty. But of course that was the problem of the fort commandante, Juan de la Vandera.

Commandante de la Vandera decided to solve his problem by the simple means of ordering the Indians to bring in provisions from their own storehouses. With this in mind, he set out one June day in 1576 to attend an Indian festival. Now it so happened that the festival was being held on our island of Escamacu. It was, Vandera reported, an island surrounded by rivers. Its soil was sandy and made very good clay for pottery and tiles. There was good earth for raising corn, too, and grapevines grew in abundance. No reason at all why the chief of Escamacu and his kinsmen could not contribute from their own plenty to the fort's need, he decided, and he called the chiefs together and told them so peremptorily. In addition, he informed them, from now on forty of the soldiers would go to live in the villages and the Indians would be expected to treat them like kings.

The chieftains apparently took the order in good grace and returned home. The soldiers were sent out to their new quarters. Father Juan in Orista heard the news with heavy heart. He knew the pride of his Indian people. This quartering of foreign troops upon them would send their hatred flaring to new heights, like a pine knot touched to embers. He heard the talk at council fires, the mutterings, the undercurrent of hatred. He dared not stay longer in the village. If he were killed, his death would only bring sure retaliation, sure warfare between his red brothers and his countrymen. So, sorrowfully he tore down the little mission so that none might desecrate it and made ready to leave. As he spoke farewell, his voice carried the tremulo of troubled overtones, and as he started down the path he turned to speak again. They had only to send for him in peace and he would come again, he said. But in his heart he knew such message would never come. He had not really touched them, for all his work, his patience and sincerity. So he left the land of Santa Elena, and there is no stone or cross to mark his mission. But perhaps someday someone digging in the soil of this island he called Escamacu may find a crucifix or rosary that the hands of Father Juan Rogel once blessed.

He left none too soon, for the Indians did go on the warpath and only a few Spaniards huddling in the fort at San Felipe were left alive. Somehow they got word to the governor at San Augustin and he sent three ships to aid them. However, the terrified widows of the slain soldiers did not want aid but only a means of escape, and the captain of the expedition finally decided to abandon the fort and take all of the setttlers away with him. So after ten years of strange ways in a new land, the story of San Felipe ended. The next year when new settlers came they decided to build a new fort on a different site and give it a new name, San Marcos (St. Mark). Here they built more than sixty houses of a substantial mixture of oyster shells and sand, later to be called "tabby" or "tappy" and widely used in all sea-island building. This fort also would last ten years and then give way before Indian assault.

Although neither of the two Spanish forts was built on our island, the Spaniards did use Escamacu for a watering place, and the name Spanish Wells is still used on the island's landward shore near the entrance to Broad Creek. The channel flowing past this shore has long been called Calibogue Sound, and the word Calibogue is very much like the Creek Indian word for deep spring—calaobe. One early map writes *"Caleboco"*— a spelling even closer to the Indian word. Early Spanish maps mark the island with the welcome words "agua dulce" and French charts bear the legend "eau douce." In any language the news of a site for fresh water would be soon translated, and we can be sure that many a sailing vessel far from home stopped to fill empty water casks on our island shores.

Sometime during the ten years that San Marcos endured, word came from friendly Guale Indians that the crew of a French ship wrecked at the harbor entrance had built a fort on the punta de Santa Elena and planned to attack the Spanish garrison. Whether this French fort was on our own island or across the harbor mouth at Bay Point will probably never be known, for the Spanish were quick to wipe out every trace of it. At length the Spanish themselves were massacred by the Indians, Spanish priests as well as Spanish soldiers, and the Jesuits sent their missionaries elsewhere. The Franciscans next took up the work of converting the Indians and went from village to village, preaching and teaching and building the crosses of wood which the Indians respected even if they did not worship them as the priests wished.

Presently the Escamacu tribe began to withdraw to the north, following their Orista kinsmen, and the Archives of the Indies began to refer to our island as "Isla de los Osos" —Island of the Bears. There were indeed bears, great, shaggy, black-furred fellows all along the coast, and this island was no exception. Whether there were more bears here than elsewhere or whether there just happened to be some bears playing at water's edge on the day a Spanish mapmaker was wondering what to name this island no one seems to know. In any case, Island of the Bears it was,without a doubt, and so it was plainly marked on the maps prepared by the pilot Andres Gonzales in 1605 under the direction of Captain Francisco Fernandez de Ecija, who also mentioned that on the island of Los Osos he conferred with a chieftain of the Escamacu and secured from him an interpreter to aid him on further exploration northward. Evidently, then, the Escamacu withdrawal from the island was a gradual migration, not a sudden evacuation, and perhaps only an attempt to find fresh hunting grounds not depleted by Spanish muskets.

In 1612 the Franciscans were still in the sea islands, Fray Luis de Oré at the head of a faithful band numbering twenty or more, but by 1617 the Archives of the Indies recorded that there was no longer a mission post at Santa Elena. By 1650 one had been opened again, but it did not last many years. The reason was not Indian opposition, but the coming of the English.

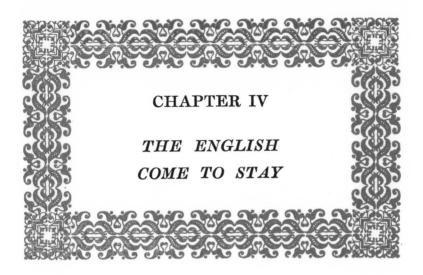

CHAPTER IV

THE ENGLISH
COME TO STAY

C HARLES THE FIRST of England was easily persuaded that those early voyages of the Cabots in 1497
gave him full claim to the whole North American
continent. True, the Catholic Pope had decreed these lands
to be Spanish, but Protestant England owed no allegiance
to His Holiness. Consequently, the English were free to
settle where they pleased, and they had pleased to settle in
Virginia and New England and several places in between.
Now they began to look southward to the tempting green
lands of Spanish Florida and Santa Elena. The land would
need a new name, of course, to go with the new owner, a
name that honored King Charles of England. From the
Latin "Carolus" they formed the name 'Carolana" soon
changed to "Carolina." It was a good choice, regardless of
whom it honored, for a Spanish king named Charles had
sponsored the land's first discovery and a French King
Charles had been the namesake of its first Protestant colony.
The English with their new Charles were the last to come
and they would be the last to leave. Carolina, north and
south, the land would remain, and the sea islands of the
Carolina shore would bear witness to their triple heritage.

In 1629 Charles the First of England bestowed the new
land of Carolana, extending from 31° to 36° north latitude
on his favored attorney general, Sir Robert Heath. Heath

did sponsor a voyage of exploration to his new domain but he did nothing about establishing colonies. While he was dilly-dallying, the English Revolution under Cromwell beheaded Charles the First. By the time the monarchy was restored and Charles the Second was on the throne, the new Charles felt he had the right to grant the land of Carolina all over again. Accordingly he did so in 1662, naming as the new owners eight Lords Proprietors: Edward, Earl of Clarendon; George, Duke of Albemarle; William, Lord Craven; John, Lord Berkeley; Anthony, Lord Ashley, later Earl of Shaftsbury; Sir George Carteret; Sir William Berkeley; and Sir John Colleton. In time through sale or inheritance the proprietorship would pass to some others, but these were the original eight. In 1665 the boundaries were extended to include from 29° to 36°30' and eventually the territory was divided into two territories, north and south.

Among the first Englishmen to eye the new Carolina land longingly were several planters in the Bermudas and Barbadoes who were feeling cramped for space in those tiny Caribbean outposts. Now there was living in the Barbadoes in the year 1663 a young sea captain named William Hilton who had already sailed on one voyage to the Carolina country near Cape Fear. As a boy he had gone with his father to the English colony at Plymouth, also, and so a more experienced man for Atlantic coastal waters would be hard to find. Consequently the planters asked him to captain a voyage of exploration to Carolina and they paid for the venture with contributions of sugar. Hoping to get grants of free land, they sent a message off to London with terms of their proposal. Hilton was ready to sail before an answer arrived, and his sponsors told him to sail without it. Someone was going to be first in South Carolina, and they might as well be the ones.

So with Captain Anthony Long and Peter Fabian as next-in-command and Pyram Bowers and John Hancock as mates, Hilton heaved anchor on his good ship *Adventure* and sailed from Speight's Bay (He wrote 'Spike's Bay" in his diary) on August 10, 1663, steering his course for the

Spanish Santa Elena, which he called Saint Ellen's in proper English. No taste of Spanish on his tongue. English land should have English names. His journal reports:

"After sixteen days of fair weather and prosperous winds, Wednesday, the 26th instant, four of the clock in the Afternoon, God be thanked, we espied Land on the coast of Florida in the latitude of 32°30', being four leagues or thereabouts to the northward of St. Ellen's, having run 550 leagues, and to the westward of the meridian of the Barbadoes 331 leagues. This evening and the night following we lay off, and Thurs-..the 27th inst. in the morning we stood in with the Land and coasted the shoar to the southward, ankering at nights and sending our boat out a-mornings, till we came into the latitude 31° but found no good harbour that way. On Sunday the 30th inst. we tacked and stood Northward and on Wednesday the 2nd of Sept. we came to anker in 5 fathoms at the mouth of a very large opening of three leagues wide or there-abouts, in the latitude 32°30' and sent our boat to sound the channel. On Thursday the 3rd we entered the Harbour (the present St. Helena Sound) and found that it was the River Jordan and was but 4 leagues north or thereabouts from Port Royal, which by the Spaniards is called St. Ellen's . . . On Saturday the fifth two Indians came aboard of us and said they were from St. Ellen's, being very bold and familiar; speaking many Spanish words, as *Capitan, camarado* and *Adeus.* They know the use of guns and are as little startled at the firing of a piece of Ordnance as he that hath been used to them many years. They told us the nearest Spaniards were at St. Augustine, and several of them had been there which they said was but 10 days journey and that the Spaniards used to come to them at St. Ellen's sometimes in canoas within the land, at other times in small vessels by sea . . . . Monday the 14th our long boat went to St. Ellen's with 12 hands. On Wednesday the 16th came 5 Indians aboard us . . ."

From these five Indians Hilton learned that the nearest Spaniards were not far away at St. Augustine but right in the Indian camp. There also were in the camp four English captives who had been shipwrecked farther up the coast. Hilton promptly showed the Indians his store of beads, hatchets, hoes and other tools and promised them that they might help themselves if only they would bring the English captives to the big ship. The Indians agreed and promised to return the following day.

But the next day no Indians appeared with captives and neither did the long boat with its crew of twelve return from St. Ellen's. Hilton grew worried. Was this tale of English captives a Spanish trick to lure the English ashore to ambush? It was not at all unlikely. The Spaniards had a very honest claim to the land they had occupied so many years and no doubt they were still seeking reprisal for the burning of St. Augustine by Sir Francis Drake in 1582. Spaniards had long memories for such offenses, and Hilton fingered his yellow beard and pondered what to do.

When another party of nine or ten Indians visited the ship he made a quick decision, seized some of them as hostages and told the rest that if they would bring him the Englishmen, their own countrymen would be freed. Presently the longboat from St. Ellen's returned, having suffered no mishap after all, and was sent out again to see if they could catch some glimpse of these English captives. The Indians reappeared, still without any Englishmen, but at last they did bring one of the castaways who told Hilton that there were not four captives, but nine more besides himself, and three others who had been killed. The Indians swore that they had only one more white man, the others had been taken to Santa Elena. Hilton evidently went to St. Ellen's to see for himself traveling by the inland waterway, for his journal reports:

"The entertainment we had at St. Ellen's put us in great fear of the Indians' treachery, for we observed their continual gathering together, and at last began with stern-look countenances to speak roughly to us and came to search our men's bandileers and pockets, yet inviting us to stay the night with them . . . That which we noted was a fair house builded in the shape of a dove house, round, 200 feet at least, completely covered with palmeta leaves and wal-plate, being 12 foot high or thereabouts, and within lodging rooms and forms; two pillars at the entrance of a high seat above all the rest. Also another house like a sentinel house, floored ten feet high with planks, fastened with spikes and nayles, standing upon substantial posts, with several other small houses round about. Also we saw many planks to the quantity of three thousand feet or thereabouts, with other timber squared, and a Cross before the Great House. Likewise we saw the ruines of an old fort, compassing more than half an acre of land within the trenches, which we supposed to be Charlesfort, built and so called by the French in 1562. (Evidently Hilton did not know about San Felipe and San Marcos forts, built more recently than the French Charlesfort.) . . .

On Monday, September 21 one English youth was brought aboard us from St. Ellen's by an Indian, who informed us that there were four more of their company at St. Ellen's, but he could not tell whether the Indians would let them come to us. For, saith he, our men told me that they had lately seen a frier and two Spanyards more at St. Ellen's who tole them they would send soldiers suddenly to fetch them away . . ."

The negotiations for the return of the captives went on for some days, during which time the Indians freely brought gifts of corn, venison, squash ("pompions," Hilton called them), deer skins and a sort of sweet wood. Then one day a sailor spied a freshly-made Spanish biscuit in an Indian's basket, and this proof of the Spaniards' nearness strengthened the fear of attack. Presently the Indians brought a letter written in Spanish, which no one could translate, but Hilton answered it in English, asking for his countrymen's release.

Captain Hilton had already released the first Indian hostages he had claimed, but now he seized two more, one of them being the son of the "King" of St. Ellen's. Then he moved the *Adventure* further up the river to a place where there was fresh water and sent a boat ashore under guard to fill the water casks. Here the Indians brought them another letter from the Spanish captain and also a letter written by one of the English captives. Much to Hilton's amazement, the Spanish captain also sent a gift—a haunch of venison and a quarter of fresh pork—more than welcome to voyagers grown understandably weary of ship's biscuits and salt meat. Was it an honest gift, or only a Spanish trick to allay their fears so they would fall easy victims to a surprise attack? The troubled Englishman did not know, but he sent a jug of English brandy as a return gift and kept his musket handy.

The Spanish captain then disclaimed any interest in the English captives—although he had traveled clear from St. Augustine to get them—and advised Hilton that he had only to give the Indians some trade goods, such as spades, axes, knives and beads, and they would be satisfied to turn over the prisoners. The large groups of Indians gathering on the shore looked more like warriors than traders, to Hilton's suspicious eye, and when the Indians assured him that the Spanish soldiers were on the way to see him, he decided that it was indeed the warpath, not a peace parley, they had in mind. Consequently he weighed anchor and moved on down the channel and when three days passed and there was no further sign of any English captives, he concluded that the Indians did not really mean to bring any others to him, and so put out to sea, Monday, September 28.

He had already explored the harbor of St. Ellen's or Port Royal from the inland waterway, and now he decided to investigate its seaward approach. Now, apparently for the first time, he saw the headland that bears his name, standing out bluff and bold at the southwest of the entrance, the perfect landmark for taking safe bearings to enter in deep water and avoid the shoals.

"The said headland is bluff," he wrote, "and seems so

steep as though trees hung over the water." Then with careful mariner's directions he went on to explain how any captain keeping the bluff headland as landmark would find all bold steering and safe entry. From that moment on it was named "Hilton Head" and so it has been called ever since, written plainly on many a sailor's chart and in many a sea journal.

From Tuesday, September the 29th, to Friday the second of October the *Adventure* cruised along the shore, and Captain Hilton took good note of all he saw. But the next day this leisurely inspection was ended abruptly by a violent storm which sent the ship scudding out to sea, and the strong current swept them nearly to Cape Hatteras. On Monday, the twelfth of October, they came to anchor at Cape Fear, which Hilton spelled "Cape Fair" in his journal, and no doubt it looked fair after such stormy seas. It was a good land, he noted, well timbered and with ample room to accommodate thousands of English settlers.

Back home in Carlisle Bay on the sixth day of January, 1664, Hilton said little of Cape Fear and much more about the land of Port Royal, the River Jordan and Edistow. This was the place to settle, he told his sponsors enthusiastically, and no doubt the written description in his journal passed from hand to hand as the eager Barbadians asked question upon question about the new land they soon hoped to call home. No wonder Hilton was enthusiastic, they decided as they read his notes:

"The lands are laden with large, tall trees—oaks, walnuts and bayes, except facing the sea it is most pines, tall and good. The land generally, except where the Pines grow, is a good soyl covered with black mold, in some places a foot, in some places, half a foot, and in other places lesse with clay underneathe mixed with the sand; and we think may produce anything as well as most parts of the Indies that we have seen. The Indians plant in the worst land because they cannot cut down the timber in the best, and yet have plenty of corn, pompions, water-mellons, musk-mellons. Although the land be overgrown with weeds through their laziness, yet they have two or three Crops of Corn a year, as the Indians themselves informed us. The Country abounds with grapes, large figs and peaches; the woods with deer, conies, turkeys, quails, curlues, plovers, teile, herons, ducks and mallard and innumerable other water fowls whose names we know not, which lie in the rivers and marshes and on the sands. Oysters in abundance with a great store of mussels. A sort of fair crabs, and a round shell fish called horsefeet. The Rivers stored plentifully with fish which we saw play and leap. There are great marshes, but most as far as we saw of little worth, except for a root that grows in them that the Indians make good bread of. (This root is of the taro family, sometimes called eddo, and includes several specimens of the aroid group, one of which is called elephant's ear. The plants still grow in island marshes.)

"The land, we suppose, is healthful, for the English that were castaway on the coast in July last were there most part of that time of year that is sickly in Virginia, and notwithstanding hard usuage and lying on the ground naked, yet had their perfect health all the time. The Natives are very healthful; we saw many very aged among them. The ayr is clear and sweet, the countrey very pleasant and delightful. And we could wish that all they that want a happy settlement of our English nation were well transported thither."

So Hilton wrote, and Anthony Long and Peter Fabian signed their names with his to show that they seconded his writings. More than one Barbadian planter was ready to start packing for the new venture, but back in England the Lords Proprietors were having a little legal trouble with the people who claimed Carolina under the old grant to Sir Robert Heath. Consequently it was 1666 before the Lords Proprietors got around to sending an expedition of their own. For some reason they had not accepted the proposals of Hilton's sponsors and wanted their own man to look over the land before they agreed to a selling price. Their man was Robert Sandford, esquire, with the rank of

Chief Register for the Proprietors, and like Hilton he kept a very interesting journal which has been saved for us as part of the "Shaftsbury Papers" and reprinted with other early journals in volume five of the South Carolina Historical Society Collections.

Like Hilton before him Sandford recognized our island headland as the best landmark for entering the channel and wrote:

" . . . the southernmost cape or headland without Port Royal called from its discoverer *Hilton Head,* which is the farthest land in sight as you come from the northeast . . . and is bluffe with trees large and tall, which as you approach them seem to looke their tops in the sea . . .

I removed opposite to the principal Indian town and there anchored before itt, where I had not ridd long ere the cassique himself come aboard mee with skins and bidding me welcome after their manner. I went ashoare with him to see their towne which stood in sight of our vessel . . . with a plaine place before the Great House for their bowling recreation, at the end of which stood a faire wooden Cross of the Spaniard's erection. But I could not observe that the Indians performed any adoration before it . . . the whole country is nothing but several small islands made by the various intervenings of the rivers and creeks, yett they are firme and good lands excepting what is marsh, nor of soe small a size but to continue, many of them, thousands of acres of rich, habitable woodland whose very bankes add such a commodiousnesse for portage as fewe countreys are equally happy in."

Reluctantly Sandford added that his group had already decided to settle at Edisto where they had first landed, but he was hard pressed not to change his mind and settle near Hilton Head, so fair did this island seem.

No doubt someone pointed out to him that Hilton Head was more open to Spanish attack, which was undeniably true. And Sandford or anyone else who tried to cozen himself into thinking that the Spanish conquistadores would yield the land without a battle was plain foolish. Nonetheless, Sandford looked back over his shoulder as they sailed away from Hilton Head, looked back wistfully at the pine-topped bluff and the harbor mouth curved like a half-bent bow and hoped that someday he would return.

Another who looked back also was Henry Woodward, a young surgeon who had come out to the Barbadoes from England just in time to start out on the venture to Carolina. Later he would ask the Indians what that island with the bluff headland was called, and they answered him in Spanish: Los Osos. When he persisted, wanting an Indian name, they had no answer. Perhaps the Indians had never had a name for the island. Possibly they had stopped calling it the island of Chief Maccou or the Escamacu because those Indians no longer lived there.

Young Woodward had plenty of time to ask his questions, for when the other Englishmen sailed back to the Barbadoes, Woodward stayed on—at his own suggestion— as a "tenant at large" for the Lords Proprietors. He found a good friend among the tribes, Shadoo, who had been taken hostage to the Barbadoes by Hilton and evidently treated well and returned to his homeland in the years between. From Shadoo and others Henry Woodward learned to speak the Indian tongue and follow Indian ways. He also learned the reason why the Indians of Port Royal were eager to have the English settle among them. They wanted the English as allies against a fierce tribe of man-eating Indians called Westoes. The Spanish soldiers, far away at St. Augustine, were no protection at all, they said. And they were right. Even before Sandford had time to return from the Barbadoes with the colonists, those fierce Westoes swarmed down upon the islands of Port Royal and all but wiped out the remaining Cusabo tribes, burning whole villages and killing men, women and children. Fortunately for Henry Woodward, he was elsewhere.

When at last the first ship with English colonists for Carolina came sailing into Port Royal Harbor, not an Indian came down to the shore to greet them. The harrying

Westoes had returned to their inland towns and the Cusabos had hidden themselves so deep in the woodlands that they did not even see the great white-sailed ships for two days. Then they came hurrying down to greet their friends the English, crying "Hiddy doddy, camarado Angles. Westo skorrye." This bit of mixed-up gibberish evidently meant that the English were good friends and the Westoes unspeakably nothing. It is amusing to speculate that "Hiddy doddy" might be the Escamacu version of "How do you do?"

Then the colonists spoke of settling there on the islands, but the Indians shook their heads, glancing over their shoulders fearfully as if a man-eating Westo might leap from the nearest thicket. Go farther north, they advised. Go north, as they themselves were doing. So the first Carolinians went on past Hilton Head to found the first English settlement of Charles Town on the Ashley River. The year was 1670. Even as the Carolinians were building their log houses, far away in Madrid the Spanish diplomats were signing a treaty with England, agreeing that the English could keep unmolested any town they had already founded. The Spaniards did not know about Charles Town when they signed the paper, and when they did find out that the English had intruded so far south into Spanish Florida they felt they had been tricked. Nevertheless, according to the wording of the treaty they had to grant that Charles Town was on English soil. But Hilton Head was not. Santa Elena was still Spanish and they intended to keep it that way. Although William Hilton probably still thought his namesake island the fairest spot in the colony he went to Charleston with the others. When he died there in 1675, Hilton Head Island was still Spanish soil and the Spaniards were ready to defend it. When Henry Woodward on one of his scouting trips to Indian country strayed south of Santa Elena, the Spaniards promptly captured him and took him prisoner to their fort at St. Augustine. Here he probably would have stayed till he died, had not the English pirate Searles raided the town and set him free. Searles carried Woodward to a port where he could take ship for the Caro-

linas and in short order he was back on his lands near
Charles Town. It was neither the first nor the last pirate
raid on the coast, and Charles Town itself would have its
fill of pirate tales in the years ahead.

Meanwhile, the Spaniards had given up the fort at Santa
Elena and had no mission north of St. Catherine's Island
off the Guale (Georgia) coast. This did not mean that they
had given up their claim to the land, but at least they were
not there in person to defend it. Consequently a band of
Scottish Covenanters under Lord Cardross thought Port
Royal a good place to found a colony where they could
have religious freedom and a very profitable Indian trade
to boot. In 1684 they built their Stuart's Town on Scot's
Island—the same island that the Spanish and French had
chosen for their first forts—and set right out to persuade the
Indians to trade with them instead of with the English at
Charles Town or the Spanish at St. Augustine. There is
some evidence that Cardross actually armed the Indians
against the Spanish and urged them to oust the dons from
Florida. However that may be, large groups of Yamassee
Indians from Florida began swarming to the Port Royal
sea island under the leadership of Chief Altamaha. Cardross
welcomed them, inviting them to settle on Hilton Head and
St. Helena Islands leaving Parris Island—Scot's Island, he
called it—for the Covenanters. So they did, and once more
the shores of Hilton Head glowed with the light of Indian
camp fires, and the bear and deer and other wild creatures
learned anew their cunning in avoiding Indian snare or
feathered arrow.

Four years the Scots and the Yamassees lived thus in
friendship and then suddenly the tall sails of Spanish warships loomed on the horizon. With loud cries for vengeance,
the Spaniards fell upon the little settlement and burned it
to the ground. Perhaps if Cardross himself had been there,
he might have rallied the Scots—or he might not. At any
rate, he was back in Scotland and the Spanish dons were the
victors.

Heady with triumph the Spanish fleet sailed on to ravage
outlying plantations between Hilton Head and Charles

Town, and massed for attack on the town itself. The winds were on the side of the Carolinians that day, for a sudden hurricane blew up from the Caribbean and scattered the Spanish ships like so many paper toys. Battered and storm-tossed, the Spanish galleons wallowed back to St. Augustine for repairs, and Charles Town relaxed. Hurricane winds were not always ill winds after all, they wrote home to England. They also wrote for aid in equipping a fleet to sail against the Spaniards, but to this plan the Lords Proprietors would not listen. Under no circumstances were the Spaniards to be aroused to further reprisal against Carolina. There was the Anglo-Spanish Treaty of Madrid, remember, and besides His Majesty had his own diplomatic reasons for wanting peace with Spain. It was a decision that Charles Town had no choice but to accept, and they turned again to building homes and raising crops.

As early as 1682 the English colonists had begun buying from the Indians some of the land around the Broad River and Port Royal Harbor, buying it more as an investment for the future than as a present homesite. Every settler who came to the colony was allowed to take up extra land for each member of his household, for each man, woman or child, each bonded servant or slave. For each one thousand pounds of sugar invested in the colony a man was allowed five hundred acres of land. Much larger acreage was granted along with the new Carolina titles of Landgrave and Cacique—given in return for some political favor—and these grants were called baronies. Much of this land must needs be claimed outside the immediate environs of Charles Town, and although fear of the Indians and Spaniards long kept settlers away from Hilton Head, the land here and elsewhere in Port Royal was eventually claimed. After all, it was excellent farming land, and the Proprietors had especially urged the settlers to plant crops "to satisfy ye belly . . . as ye foundation of yr Plantation." Planting of cotton, indigo and ginger roots, sesame seed, sugar cane, grape vines and olive sets, orange, lemon and lime seedlings had all been brought from their old homes in the Barbadoes. From the Indians they purchased corn, beans, peas, turnips, carrots and potatoes for planting. There was also much talk of raising silkworms, for the mulberry trees which furnished their natural food grew everywhere in the Carolina country. But any of these crops took time to grow and the colonists turned to the shipping of naval suplies for a readier profit: beams and masts from the tall trees of the forest, pine tar, turpentine, pitch. Another ready profit came from cattle-raising, and the sea islands provided a good, nourishing cattle range, safely "fenced" by the sea. Pigs did well on the islands, too, growing fat on acorns. Untended, they both became more than half wild, free-roaming companions for the wild marsh tackeys descended from the horses the Spaniards had left behind.

Apparently the first white man actually to live on any of the Port Royal Islands after the disastrous burning of Stuart's Town was the famous Indian trader, Thomas Nairne, but the warrant for his land claim on St. Helena has been lost. The first recorded claim went to John Stuart, another Indian trader, who took one thousand acres of St. Helena early in 1698. On August 12 of that same year Major Robert Daniell, the justly admired statesman and soldier, claimed the 3,020 acres of Scot's Island and all of Port Royal Island as part of the 48,000 acres granted to him with his new title of landgrave.

Now Hilton Head entered the list. On August 16, 1698, it was included as part of the barony granted to John Bayley of Ballingclough in the County of Tipperary in the Kingdom of Ireland who had just been dubbed landgrave and cacique. Landgrave Bayley spread his 48,000 acre claim over several parishes, taking land both on the sea islands and on the mainland along the Santee River.

Neighboring islands were soon claimed also. Colonel Alexander Mackey, another Indian trader, bought the island nearest to Hilton Head on the northwest and the stream between it and the mainland would be known as Mackey's Creek for many years to come, although Mackey's Island eventually yielded to the new title of Pinckney's Island. Apparently it was an old Indian stronghold, for the words "Ruins of Indian Fort" are marked on the northern tip of

Chalices Dated 1834; Used in Episcopal Zion Chapel of Ease

Thomas Henry Barksdale, 1795-1832 — *Miniature by Antoine Meucci. Photo courtesy of Mrs. G. A. Kalber*

Ferry *Pocahontas* Used From 1953 to 1956
Orion D. Hack

Mackey Island on a map drawn by Captain John Gascoigne, who bought land in Bayley's Barony in 1729 and no doubt saw the ruins. A man named Pinney bought Spanish Point on Scot's Island in 1699 and Daniell sold the rest to Edward Archer in 1701. Archer sold to Col. Alexander Parris in 1715, and it was he who gave that island the name by which it is still known. Parris gave 1,320 acres to his daughter Jane and her husband John de la Bere as a wedding settlement in 1715. Two other families, the Barnwells and the Hatters, had been there since 1704. By 1706 there were enough settlers so that there was talk of establishing a garrison and fort to protect them against Indian or Spanish attack. No fort was built, but stores of ammunition and piles of kindling for signal beacons were cached on the islands along the inland waterway as far south as Savannah River. In that very year a combined French and Spanish attack was made on Charleston without much success but with certain proof that the Spanish had not yet given up Santa Elena.

There was still constant threat of Spanish attack when the town of Beaufort was founded in 1711 at the mouth of Port Royal River opposite Lady's Island (now spelled Ladies', but originally "Our Lady's" to honor the Virgin Mary). This new town, third to be founded in the colony, was in Granville County, a new division of the older Colleton County and named in honor of Lord Granville, a new Proprietor. Several families in the county having signified their willingness to build and support an Episcopal church there, the new parish of St. Helena was created to serve Beaufort and the surrounding sea islands and countryside. Although religious freedom for all had been one of the original principles in the Carolinas, and many Huguenot, Covenanter, Quaker and Jewish families had come there and been freely accepted, the Anglican Episcopal Church was the official religion. Therefore the Episcopal Church parishes were official districts and would be so until the last of the next century.

Hilton Head Island, St. Helena Parish, Granville County in the colony of South Carolina apparently still did not have a house built on it, for all its imposing address, and neither did Beaufort Town. Threat of Indian attack was a real danger in any part of the colony and there was small sense in building a home where there was threat of Spanish attack as well. The Indians were trouble enough, although the colonists had no one but themselves to blame for Indian hostility. In the beginning the Indians had been more than willing to be friends. In return the Carolinians had taken their land, paying for it with only a few beads, a knife, a hatchet; and then had added cause for hatred by taking Indian slaves. They repeatedly egged rival tribes into fighting each other so that the captives would furnish a never-ending supply for the slave market. Slavery was a part of the Carolina way of life from the beginning. The settlers had brought Negro slaves with them from the Barbadoes and they could not vision managing their vast plantations without slave labor. Negroes worked better than Indians, they agreed, but the red men were more available.

In 1712 the officials persuaded the remaining Indians in the Port Royal islands to move to Polawana Island, where many of them had already withdrawn. This land was supposed to be theirs and their children's after them forever more, but even the Indians did not really believe such a promise by this time. If the Indians were left undisturbed, it was only because the white man had other things to do.

War was in the air. Both Spain and France were potential enemies and Carolinians kept sharp lookout to seaward. Scout boats were equipped to patrol the inland waterway. One boat cruised from Beaufort to the Stono and the other went past Hilton Head Island with orders to keep a lookout clear to St. Augustine. Besides looking for warships the scouts also had the task of capturing runaway slaves, and of course there was always a chance of sighting a pirate ship. For the most part, Carolinians had long followed a policy of "live and let live" with the pirates, selling them naval stores and food supplies so long as they had gold to pay for them. Of course this did not meet official approval and in 1692 Capt. Robert Seabrook, whose descendants would later live on Hilton Head, was fined for "unlawful commerce with

ye pyratts and selling them provisions and arms." Lawful
or not, the commerce went on, and most of the coins in cir-
culation in the colony had been brought there by the pirates
and privateers. The only coin put out by the Lords Proprietors was more of a medal than money, although it was rated
at the worth of a half-penny. It was copper and bore the
picture of an elephant and the date 1694 with the legend
"God save Carolina and the Lords Proprietors." Colony
officials had captured a few pirates and hanged them, and
others had turned honorable gentlemen and accepted the
King's Grace in 1701. However, it seemed by the year 1715
that the "Grace" had lost its potency and the pirates were
feeling a strong urge to hoist the skull-and-crossbones ban-
ner once again. The sea islands with their crossing creeks
and rivers offered good haven to them and it is very likely
that more than one pirate vessel took shelter on Hilton
Head Island, although it was apparently not the headquarters for any one band. Nevertheless, pirates did use sea-
island hideaways to careen their ships and plot new ven-
tures, and the words "Careening Point" are marked on old
maps of Hilton Head by the banks of Skull Creek. Tradition says that Skull Creek was originally named "Skulk"
because Indians skulked along its banks before attacking
settlers. Nineteenth century maps more peaceably labeled
it *Scull* Creek. However, the more frequent spelling is
Skull, and proof that this is the right choice is found on old
maps that put the word "Golgotha" on the creek shore near
Careening Point, for *golgotha* is derived from the Hebrew
word for skull. Perhaps the pirates skulked here, as well
as Indians, and left skulls behind them as witnesses to evil.
Did they leave buried treasure also? Spanish doubloons and
milled dollars, Portuguese half-joanas, English guineas,
French louis-d'ors, the silver coins of faraway Peru and
Mexico? That—so far—is one of the island's unanswered
questions.

In 1715 the rallying war cry of the Yamassee Indians
made the people of Port Royal forget pirates and everything else. Trouble began inland with the massacre of
Thomas Nairne and other Indian agents. Luckily, a wounded

man and a boy managed to escape and ran to the islands with warning. Just in time the settlers managed to flee, snatching only the dearest of their treasures as they fled, and raced to the safety of a ship anchored in the harbor. The ship had lately been seized for smuggling, but now it was a heaven-sent means of escape to Charleston. Eventually the Yamassee were defeated and withdrew to St. Augustine, where they had already sent their women and children to await them—proof enough that the Spaniards there had connived at the attack. Supposedly that was the end of Yamassee warpaint but as late as 1728 a war party of Yamassee braves landed across Calibogue Sound on Daufuskie Island and gave the spot its name of Bloody Point by massacreing the whole crew of the Beaufort Scout boat and carrying Captain Gilbert to the Spanish prison at St. Augustine.

The end of the war opened all the former Yamassee lands to settlement and made it much safer to live on the sea islands, although the Spanish were still to be counted as enemies. There would be another Indian uprising in 1733 and another in 1739, with a slave revolt in the latter year as well, and all were blamed on the Spaniards. But that first peaceful summer of 1717 things looked promising on the Carolina coast and seventy town lots were taken up in Beaufort. Even Hilton Head was now considered safe, for John Barnwell claimed a grant of five hundred acres on the island's northwest corner on December 10, 1717. Evidently this had not been a part of Bayley's Barony, possibly because it was well separated by marsh or high tides. So far as we know, he has good claim to the title of Hilton Head's first settler.

About this time Mr. Alexander Trench and wife Hester arrived in Carolina from Dublin, Ireland. They took lodgings in Charleston and later came to Beaufort and bought half of town lot No. 69, with Edward Wigg as co-owner. This Alexander Trench was out to make his fortune in the new world, for he immediately began investing in cattle, trade goods and land, and was listed as both merchant and attorney. His main role was that of agent for John

Bayley, son and heir of Landgrave John Bayley of Ballingclough in the county of Tipperary in the kingdom of Ireland. Son John wanted to dispose of the wild Carolina country he had inherited, and Trench took over the task. The
agent must have been his own best customer, for he bought
all of Whitehall Plantation across from Beaufort and a
large piece of Bayley land in Rapphoe Barony along the
Santee River. Whether he also bought or leased the Bayley
land on Hilton Head is not clear, but he did use the island
for grazing his cattle and it soon became known locally as
"Trench's Island." When the English sea captain John
Gascoigne bought land from Agent Trench in June, 1729,
the tract was described thus: (Memorial Bk. I, p. 398).

. . . . plantation containing 500 acres in St. Helena
Parish, Granville County, part of an island commonly
known by the name Trenches Island, butting and
bounding south on Roger Moor, east on marsh join-
ing to the back creek, west on marsh and a creek out of
Dawfuskee River, north on said Trench, . . . said
500 acres part of landgrave patent dated 16 August,
1698 unto John Bayley. . . .

The wording "commonly known as" in the above listing
does not prove ownership, but it does establish the asso-
ciation of man and place, and indeed six months earlier
when Trench drew up his will (January, 1729) he refers
to the cattle there as "being only mine upon the island." A
widely-copied map drawn by Gascoigne about 1750 labeled
Hilton Head "Trenches Island" and so the name stayed
alive on maps and sea charts in many languages and was
sometimes translated like a common noun, as in the French
"Ile de trancheèes." British war maps of the American Revolution used "Trench's Island" and so did a war map published by L. Prang & Co. of Boston as late as 1861, although
more accurate sources had long since restored the name of
Hilton Head.

Since the Gascoigne map also labels the present Jenkin's
Island as "John's" this may very well be the site of his own
claim. The main part of Hilton Head ("said Trenches") is

roughly the north boundary as described and marsh and creeks lie east and west. The listing of Roger Moor's land as southern boundary line gives us another name to place among the island's earliest settlers. The name Moor (e) does appear later in Moorefield Plantation on the mainland near Buckingham Landing. Although Gascoigne's daughter Anne remained in Carolina, married William Greenwood and lies buried in St. Philip's churchyard, Gascoigne himself returned to England. The South Carolina *Gazette* for Feb. 2, 1733, advertised his Hilton Head plantation thus: "For sale: Hog Island . . . residence . . . orange, apple, peach, nectarine, and plumb trees . . ."

Mistress Hester Trench had already left her husband a widower when he wrote his will in 1729, and so Alexander left all he possessed to his young son Frederick. The will was probated in 1733 and the estate administered by Alexander's brother the Councillor Frederick Trench of Dublin, Ireland, according to the dead man's wish. To his two executors Trench bequeathed a full suit of mourning clothes, and he also requested that his pew in St. Helena Church, Beaufort, be kept "For the use of any strangers that are not inhabitants, but transient persons." Although the pew itself was burned many years ago when most of the church was destroyed, anyone from Hilton Head Island should surely feel that he has a personal invitation from Alexander Trench himself to enter there and worship. His grave is not there, but in Charleston, where he asked to be buried beside his wife. His executors were John Wright and Benjamin Whitaker of Charleston and his witnesses were John Wallis, John Lining and Peter Shepherd. Since the name Wallis is listed among the earliest residents of Hilton Head, we can perhaps risk a guess that they were of the same family as John Wallis the witness.

Ten years later a Frederick Trench bought town lot No. 74 in Beaufort, but whether this was Alexander's son is not recorded. At any rate the Trench family apparently had no further claim to land on Hilton Head and since Alexander had not sold much of the Bayley land thereon, the official description in land transactions right up to the next century was "Hilton Head Island in Bayley's Barony." Strangely enough no headland, road, bay or creek preserves the Bayley name, and that of Alexander Trench has also been without memorial. The names of first-settlers Barnwell, Gascoigne and Moor are likewise forgotten.

In the years following Trench's death many families came to Hilton Head but, because all Beaufort County records were destroyed by war in 1864 and again by fire in 1883, the complete list of landholders will probably never be known. Such names as we have come from the parish register, from birth and death notices in the Charleston papers, from family records, articles in the *South Carolina Historical and Genealogical Magazine*, the records of the South Carolina Historical Commission and other documents on file in Charleston and Columbia.

Old maps also add to the list of residents. A map drawn by James Cook in 1766—"approved by Mr. Joiner, twenty years a pilot of that place"—adds the marginal note that there were twenty-five families living on Hilton Head in that year.

The Sayre and Bennett map of 1775 shows five houses along Skull Creek but names only two families: Wallis and Green. Another family named Greene (with an "e") is reported by other sources. One of the Greens (or Greenes) had a daughter Elizabeth and we can guess that she was the namesake for "Elizabeth Point" on the Sayre and Bennett map, the same place we call Bobb's Island. This seems especially likely when we read in the St. Helena Parish register that Elizabeth Green (e) of Hilton Head married Jeremiah Sayre (also spelled Sear) on November 20, 1770, the Reverend Mr. Pearce officiating. The Wallis home could be that of John Wallis, the witness to the Trench will, as we mentioned, or it could have belonged to Richard Wallis or Wallace, Justice of the Peace for Granville County in 1756. Farther down the shore is the Mongin (Mungen) plantation at Spanish Wells, possibly Roger Moor's old land, and still farther south is the name Ash. In a few years one of the Ash daughters would marry George Barksdale of Christ Church Parish, and the young couple would set up housekeeping on this same site. Their land lay along the public road which crossed the island from Port Royal to Calibogue Sound and bisected the south end of the island much as the paved highway now does. This map calls the southern tip "Calibogue Point." Later maps named it "Braddock's Point" and this is the name that remains today. It was evidently changed in honor of Daniel Cutler Braddock of Beaufort, captain of the scout boat. Braddock saw service in the war against the Spaniards in 1740 and in November 1742 he took Captain Gibson's place as head of the Beaufort scout galley. He stayed on duty till Christmas 1747, and went on irregular patrols up to 1764 when the treaty with Spain made further scouting unnecessary. From this date on, England had clear title to the Port Royal Islands and the Georgia territory. Whether Braddock retired to a home on Hilton Head is not clear, but he undoubtedly used the point many times as a lookout post and perhaps kindled a beacon fire there to warn the planters that a Spanish warship had been sighted. One column of smoke for each ship sighted was the agreed signal in those years of constant danger, and you can be sure that families on Hilton Head breathed lighter when there was no longer need for such warning.

On the Gascoigne maps drawn about this same time, our Calibogue Sound is labeled Dewfoskey Sound, or sometimes D'Awfoskee or other weird variations of the usual Daufuskie. Three plantations are indicated along Skull Creek: Mount Pleasant, Marabuoy and Eden. The last evidently refers to William Eden, still a landholder in 1793. Bobb's Island is Skull Island, and the stream separating it from the rest of Hilton Head is called Bear Creek—the only reminder that the whole island was once "Los Osos." The present Jenkin's Island is John's or John's Island and the tip of it often known as Hogg's (or Hog's) Island is unnamed. John and James Hogg did live in Granville County about this time, but so did plenty of wild pigs and either spelling is possible. Among the names still in use today found on this map of one hundred and eighty years ago are these: Spanish Wells, Dolphin Head, Bass Head, Fish

Baynard Family Mausoleum, Zion Chapel Cemetery

Kenneth Rogers

Cast Iron Caskets Used by Plantation Owners

Orion D. Hack

Creek, Skull Creek, Scarborough Head, Hilton Head.

On some copies the earlier alternate for Dolphin Head is *Balinclough*, a name no doubt harking back to Landgrave John Bayley of Ballingclough in Tipperary. Perhaps a confusion with *baleen*, the old word for whalebone, led to the later name.

Charleston newspapers of the 1750's tell us of some of the happenings on Hilton Head. Jacob and Elizabeth Neal had four children born to them: little Jacob on St. Patrick's Day 1753, Elizabeth on August 28, 1754 Abraham on August 8, 1756, and Sarah on May 10, 1758. Daniel Savage a widower, married on July 2, 1754, Miss Jane McKee, whose parents David and Mary lived in Granville County. Savage Island on the May River opposite Bluffton is probably named for Daniel's family. Then from Bermuda there came William and Mary Palmer to live on Hilton Head and their daughter Mary was born here January 14, 1755. Probably they did not stay long, for William was drowned only two years later. Another island couple, John and Mary Rankin, welcomed the baby Christopher on July 25, 1756, and the boy would grow to manhood on the island and fight for independence. The Bull family were living here also in these years. Arthur Bull, a planter, died on Hilton Head Christmas Day 1757, and various other references to the family will be found in the following years.

Perhaps the most important news of the next decade— and sure evidence of new settlers—was the dividing of St. Helena Parish. The new parish, St. Luke's, included Hilton Head. However, a new church building was not to be erected for another twenty years and so the parishioners of St. Luke's went on attending St. Helena's in Beaufort whenever they were in town and recorded their births, marriages and deaths in that church register. In 1760 the original Barnwell grant on the island's northwest corner was sold. John Barnwell had willed it to his daughter Bridgett in 1724 and she bequeathed it to her husband Robert Sams. Their son Robert inherited it in 1760, but died within the year, and the land was sold by his brothers to settle the estate, with the southern boundary described as "Land not laid out." New owners were William and Phoebe Jenkins Waight and the land would pass to their daughter Phoebe and her husband William Elliott. Scanning the newspapers again, we learn that Joseph Parmenter of Hilton Head died November 14, 1763, leaving his widow Sarah. In the same year Elisha and Elizabeth Tailer (Taylor) christened their baby Elizabeth. In 1769 their neighbor Jonathan Thomas died and his three slaves were appraised at a value of £732.2.6 by his neighbors Thomas Bull, David Adams and Richard Bland. The latter married Spinster Elizabeth Fendin that same year and the families of both bride and groom were island residents. Other island names on deeds and records of the 1760's are Lancelot and George Bland, Joseph and Susannah Sealy, John and James Hogg.

About this same time there came to Hilton Head the four Davant (Devant, Divant) brothers, John, James, Isaac and Charles. They were the sons of John Davant, formerly of Edisto, a man of French Huguenot and English ancestry, and the family would be closely bound with island history for the next fifty years. Evidently their first plantation was "Point Comfort," which lay at the south end between Broad Creek and the Atlantic. As the brothers married and built new homes, and as their sons and daughters married and settled nearby, an island traveler might expect to see Davant kinfolk anywhere along the public road from Braddock's Point to Port Royal.

John Davant, Jr., married twice, but left only one child, a daughter named Sarah who married John Grimball.

Isaac Davant and his wife Tabitha had son Isaac born on Hilton Head November 19, 1772.

James Davant married Lydia Page in 1769 and both are buried in the island graveyard. They had eight children, six of whom lived to maturity, and numerous grandchildren, of whom we shall read as they take their place in island affairs.

Charles, the youngest son, married Elizabeth Fendin Bland, young widow of his friend and neighbor Richard Bland, and probably lived on the plantation later known as

"Gardner's." Their only son, also named Charles, was born on Hilton Head August 23, 1779 and lived here till 1835, when he moved to Woodlawn Farm on the mainland near Gillisonville.

The 1770's add other names and events: Widow Sarah Parmenter married Lewis Bona here in June 1774, and their daughter Ann Agnes was born January 20, 1776. Just where they lived is not certain, but a place on the south end near Long Island and the entrance to Broad Creek is still called Boney's or Bunnay's Ditch. Whether this title is a twisted form of Bona or refers to the pirate Stede Bonnet can only be discussed and never decided. Of the Green (or Greene) clan, Benjamin died here in 1768 and Nathaniel and Samuel in 1770. Since newspapers and deed recorders were very careless with that final "e," the two families cannot always be separated without much research. Samuel left a son Samuel and two daughters, Sarah and Susan, and they were apparently of the family without the distinguishing "e". The will mentions the family home, "where I now live on the north side of Fish Haul Creek." By 1777 one daughter and the son were dead and the only Green heir was Sarah, wife of Thomas Tucker. Her valuable inheritance included forty-six slaves appraised at £18,900. Very likely this is the time when the Drayton family first came to Hilton Head and bought Fish Haul Plantation, sometimes called "Fish Hall." They owned a great deal of land in the area and were justly prominent socially and politically. William Drayton the elder was born in South Carolina in 1733 and although he was educated for the law in England became an ardent speaker for independence and eventually the first United States district judge. The Draytons of Fish Haul were to play an important part in island affairs.

Sometime in these same years there came to the Carolinas from Dublin, Ireland, one Henry Talbot, brickmaker and lighthouse builder. His father, Sir John Talbot, had been Lord Mayor of Dublin and no doubt heard of Hilton Head from Councillor Frederick Trench. Henry was an able businessman and soon secured a contract to build a brick lighthouse on Tybee Island off Savannah harbor and other lighthouses elsewhere along the coast. As part of his fee he was given land on Hilton Head, including a small island in Skull Creek formerly known as Delegal's Island. Possibly one of the grants was the plantation known as Brickyard or Shipyard. The other was on Skull Creek. Since Henry Talbot already had a home on Whale Branch near Beaufort he gave the Hilton Head land along Skull Creek to his younger son John, who married one of the Ladson sisters and built a home on the new land. By strange mischance, when the deed was recorded in the Colonial Land Office in London, the surname was spelled *Talbird*. Since the land was recorded in that name, Henry now began using the incorrect spelling himself, and his sons John and Thomas did likewise. Their sister Mary married the prominent Dr. John Rhodes, lately come to the Carolinas from Shropshire, England, and so was no longer troubled by the new spelling. Thomas Talbot-Talbird married Christian Crawford in 1780 and continued living in St. Helena Parish, where the births of nine children are recorded. Both brothers occasionally used the correct spelling of their name, as well as the changed form, and the name "Talbot Field" has clung to the meadows along the road to Seabrook Landing all these years. It is an historical site that deserves a marker, for here occurred an act of war of the American Revolution.

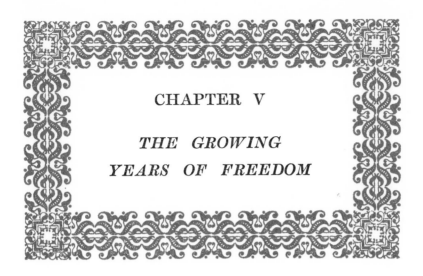

CHAPTER V

THE GROWING
YEARS OF FREEDOM

T HE SPIRIT of independence had not passed by
Hilton Head, for all its remoteness. Almost to a
man the islanders were passionately Whig Patriots in their allegiance, while on neighboring Daufuskie
Island the residents were hotly Tory, earning for it the
nickname "Little Bermuda." Hilton Head planters, with
their rich harvests of indigo ready to bring premium prices
in London markets, had as good reasons as those on Daufuskie to be loyal to Britain, but the hope for independence
was stronger than their wish for gain. So it was that while
the battles raged from Bunker Hill to Yorktown, Hilton
Head and Daufuskie islanders fought out the revolution in
miniature between themselves. And with the British fleet
besieging Charleston and Savannah, there was every reason
to think that England and the Tories would be victorious.
Blockading British warships could be sighted any day from
any island lookout, and the island was too abundantly pro-
visioned not to make a prompt target for foraging parties.
Some of the husbands and fathers of Hilton Head felt they
were needed more at home than at the front. However,
most of the able-bodied men who did not enlist in the regular army did serve with a Partisan Band, like Marion's
famous fighters. And all of them, able-bodied or not, kept
a sharp lookout for raiding parties from Daufuskie.

Charleston fell to the Redcoats in 1780 and the Patriot soldiers defending it were carried off to British prison ships in Charleston Harbor. A number of the prisoners were from Hilton Head families, and among them was young Lieutenant John Talbird. Word came to the island that he was also seriously wounded.

At home on Hilton Head his wife heard the news with heavy heart. It would have been a happy time for her if only John were safe, for there was a baby on the way. The child was born on the fateful day of Cornwallis's surrender —although the momentous news had not, of course, reached Hilton Head—October 19, 1781. The baby was named Henry for his grandfather, as his soldier-father wished, and his mother was busier than ever keeping the plantation in good order and tending her small son.

Family letters tell us that one day Mistress Talbird was startled by the sound of tramping feet. She looked up. British Redcoats were marching up the path! At the officer's order they broke ranks and began kindling a fire, lighting pine torches. They were going to burn the house! Quickly she thrust the baby into his nurse's arms and sent the slave woman running to the woods to hide. Turning to face the British officer, the mother's eyes widened in disbelief. He was her own sister's husband. With clipped military phrases he made shamefaced explanation. His orders were to burn all Patriot houses between Beaufort and Savannah. What could a soldier do but obey? However, no one had ordered him not to remove the household furniture first, and so he told the slaves to pile their mistress's possessions under a large oak tree about one hundred and fifty yards from the house. The slaves' eyes rolled in terror and black hands trembled, but the furniture was moved. The moment the work was done, the soldiers set fire to the house and then drove the slaves to the ship as fair prize of war. Along with hundreds of others captured on ravaged plantations they were later sold in the West Indies.

Fortunately a few Talbird slaves at work in the fields had managed to hide from the British and they soon built their mistress a cabin thatched with palmetto leaves, where she and the baby lived till Lieutenant John finally returned home to them. She could have spared herself those months of hardship by turning Tory, but Carolina patriots are born with stout hearts and she held fast to her loyalty and her land.

Although some of the Talbird property was sold in 1784, the family lived in their new house on Skull Creek till well after the turn of the century. Son Henry grew up an avid reader with a hankering for tinkering in his chemical laboratory. His son—also named Henry—was born on the island about 1810. Family burials, however, were usually made in the plantation on Whale Branch.

After the Talbird house burning, Hilton Head Patriots kept closer watch than before, certain that other raiding parties would follow. One night the message came that the Tories on Daufuskie were planning to attack. Word passed swiftly from one plantation to the next and grim-faced men saddled their horses and rode to the rendezvous on the southwest shore. Just across Calibogue Sound they could glimpse the shoreline of Daufuskie, and they strained to catch the sound of muffled oars. All the cold night through they waited, arms at the ready, but no one came. At last, weary and chilled, they rode back to their homes in the early winter dawn. Charles Davant and John Andrews rode side by side, ahead of the others, apparently having farther to go. They were almost at the center of the island, just where the road turns to circle the headwaters of Broad Creek. A hundred yards or so beyond the turn stood two ancient oaks with wideflung branches draped in ghostly Spanish moss. Was something moving in their shadow? Charles Davant leaned forward to see more clearly. A shot rang out. Andrews wheeled his horse and galloped back to rally the others, but Charles Davant crumpled in the saddle, a bullet in his breast. His terrified horse reared and plunged, then broke into a wild gallop for home. Clinging to the saddle, Charles had one brief glimpse of a leering, triumphant face and recognized his murderer—Martinangel of Daufuskie. Somehow he managed to keep the name on his lips while the galloping horse raced up the lane and came to a trembling halt in the dooryard.

There on the piazza he saw his son rubbing his eyes sleepily, roused by the shot at Two Oaks. With a scream of terror the lad ran to catch his father's blood-stained body as it slipped from the saddle. "Martinangel," the dying lips murmured. "Get Martinangel . . ."

Charles Davant was only a boy, but he swore a man's oath. He would kill his father's murderer. He might have to wait till he grew bigger, but he would kill him.

The men on Hilton Head were not waiting for Charles to grow to manhood. In late December of that year 1781 they called a meeting of their Partisan Band, the Bloody Legion, and took revenge in their own hands. Their leader was John Leaycraft (or Leecroft), probably the grandson of the sea captain of the same name who came from the Bermudas to marry a Charleston girl in 1752, and son of the John Leaycraft whose sloop *Charleston* went down in the violent storms of 1771.

With him were men of other island Patriot families: James Davant, of course. Lewis Bona, who had married the Widow Parmenter. John Bull, John Mongin, Senior, and his son John, also. Christopher Rankin, who had been born on Hilton Head in 1756. Daniel Savage. William Scott. Other members of the Legion, as reported in the Charlestown *Royal Gazette* for Wednesday, January 30, 1782, were: James Allan, Israel Andrews, Isaac Bolder (perhaps misspelled for Isaac Baldwin), William Cheswell, Isaac Davids, James and John Erving, John Fendin, Charles Floyd, Nathaniel Gimbal, Patrick McMullin Meredith Rich, Thomas Roberts and David Ross. If this latter group were not actually living on Hilton Head, they must have lived very close by in order to be on call for a band head-quartered here. Supervising their plantations by day and going stealthily to rendezvous by night, they had long been doing their best to harry the British troops. This particular December foray was different from the others. Their target was one man—the man named murderer by Charles Davant's last breath.

According to the Charlestown *Gazette*, published by the

occupying British forces and therefore anti-Partisan, the Bloody Legon was a "gang of banditti" and "Wretches," but the editor of the *South Carolina Historical and Genealogical Magazine* headlined his reprint of the affair "Extracts from Carolina Newspapers Regarding *Soldiers* of South Carolina in the Revolution." (Volume V, p. 59). The Legion plundered the Martinangels of nearly all they had and killed Captain Martinangel, reported the *Gazette,* no doubt correctly. Wars are made up of killings and plunderings. But whether the killers were murdering wretches or heroes depends on the point of view. To support the military status of the affair is the fact that both Charles and James Davant were paid for militia service in 1779, 1780 and 1781 and James also had pay vouchers for the following year. As witness to character is the fact that John Leaycraft stood before the altar at St. Helena's in Beaufort on June 4, 1786, and pledged security for his godson, John Leaycraft Agnew. It is not likely that any wretch from a gang of banditti would have been allowed to do so.

Oddly enough there were still Martinangels living on Daufuskie in that same year—Isaac and Elizabeth. Their daughter Mary was born there April 24, 1787. Perhaps by that time Whig and Tory animosity had been put aside.

In these years after the Revolution, the sale of land on Hilton Head seemed to be in the hands of one Peter Bayley, the heir of the orignal landgrave. Evidently agent Alexander Trench had not finished disposing of the land before his death. Furthermore, Peter Bayley was having difficulties with the way the land was developed. There is record of a lawsuit in which Bayley charged that His Excellency Benjamin Guerard had "declined" planting his grant of 1700 acres on Hilton Head. In February, 1784, the suit was noted in the South Carolina *Gazette and Public Advertiser* and by December it was still not settled. Later the same suit was continued by Benjamin Bayley, agent for Henry Bayley of Tipperary, Peter's brother and heir. When Guerard died, the lands were advertised for sale: "those famed, healthy and pleasantly located indigo lands on Scull Creek."

Actually there were three Guerard plots: one of 315 acres, described as lying between Scull and Crooked (now Jarvis) Creek, could be the present Jenkins Island or the plantation later called Fairfield. The second comprised 404 acres and lay mid-island between Broad Creek and the Atlantic. The third totalled one thousand acres, but the boundaries are not clear. "Enough for four plantations," the advertisement read.

Now Benjamin Bayley began advertising the sale of other plots from Bayley's Barony on Hilton Head, mentioning lots numbered 4, 11, 12, 13, 14, 28, 33 and 38. His headquarters were in Charleston, and eager customers soon sought him out. James Davant added No. 38—some 270 acres fronting the beach—to the land he already owned on the south end. One of the witnesses to the transaction was William Baynard who bought 265 acres of No. 12 (Muddy Creek Place) for himself. William Pope bought No. 4— 286 acres bounded by his own land on the west, by the ocean on the east, the Elliotts to the north and the Reverend Graham to the south. John Stoney bought No. 13 and No. 14, 422 acres bounded on the east by the plantation of Colonel Garden (Gardner). Axtell Hutchinson bought the 326 acres of No. 28 for £155 sterling.

On the island's northern end William and Jane Scott acquired 365 acres on the inland side of Coggins Point from William and Sarah Pope, who kept the rest of the plantation for themselves as family inheritance for generations to come. Their son, James Pope, was born on Hilton Head January 6, 1786.

These indeed were growing years on Hilton Head, with new brides and new babies mentioned frequently in Charleston papers and the parish register at St. Helena's. Richard and Rachel Capers baptized their baby son Charles on January 7, 1785. William and Mary Mongin had a baby daughter Elizabeth on December 30, 1786. James Andrew Mongin married Martha Bull in November, 1786. Still another Mongin man, Daniel, brought his bride to the island in 1798, the former Schepelia Rivers. Evidently the Spanish Wells Plantation supported all the Mongin clan, although they did eventually move to Daufuskie. Wherever they lived, they must have been prosperous, for the nickname "Money Mongin" clung to the head of the famliy for some years.

Jeremiah Sayre and his wife Elizabeth Green had a baby girl named Sarah Bell in March, 1786. Other island residents were William Hobkirk, Mrs. Katherine Hazard, James McCullough, Isaac Fripp, Captain James Doharty, John McHardie—a carpenter—and the Baldwins. Isaac and Martha Baldwin had two daughters: Sarah, born December 6, 1789, and Mary, born December 9, 1793. Mary would grow to a pretty girl, marry James Kirk and bear a son named for his father. All three of them, and other Kirks as well, are buried in the island graveyard that lies near Two Oaks where Charles Davant was murdered. The church that once stood beside it has been destroyed, but the gravestones are still there, shaded by ancient, moss-hung oaks and bright-leafed magnolias.

The names and dates engraved on those gravestones are:

Baldwin, Isaac (1752-1826), wife Martha (1771-1826), their daughter Sarah (1789-1806), daughter Mary Kirk (1793-1851).

Barksdale, Thomas Henry (1795-1832), son of George and Ann.

Baynard, William E. (The crypts in this mausoleum had been robbed before a record was made. A coffin plate found there reads "Mrs. C. A. Baynard, died May 29, 1856." This was probably Catherine Adelaide, wife of William).

Broughton, Catherine, wife of Peter (1788-1836).

Davant, James, Senior (1744-1803), wife Lydia (1755-1795). Mary, wife of James, Junior (1788-1818), their sons Samuel (Feb.-Mar. 1808), John (May-June 1818). Martha (1781-1818). Robert, son of John (1805-1808).

Flinn, James B. (1784-1812).

Irvine, William (1771-1817), his wife Mary (1762-1821).

Kirk, James, Senior (1780-1850), his wife Mary Baldwin (1793-1851), Dr. James (1825-1858), husband of Gabriella, their daughter Florence (1852-1853), Rollia (1818

-1854), William Isaac (1808-1810), two unnamed infants, 1812, 1817, James Lycurgus (1817-1823), Elizabeth (1830-1845), Benjamin (1811-1815), Octavia (1815-1821).

Roberts, B. S. born Alfred, Maine, 1819, died 1890.

Schwarzer, Paul, (1853-1905).

Sealy, James, (1817-1819).

Wagner, Charles (1840-1922).

Webb, Samuel (1799-1836), his wife Lovina (1799-1821), son William (1820-22), Thomas (1770-1816).

In addition there are these headstones in family burying grounds on the plantations:

Fyler, Dr. Samuel (1780-1821), Mary Ann (1810-1815), Aurelia (1811-1813), Seabrook Plantation.

Stoney, James (1772-1827) Drayton Plantation. Family letters reveal that John and John S. Stoney are buried here also, but their graves are unmarked.

There may be other family burial plots not yet discovered. A few graves are in the cemetery next to the chapel at Honey Horn Plantation, but these are of the last century. Yankee soldier graves were all supposedly moved to the National Cemetery in Beaufort. One shaft remains forgotten among the thickets along the road to Fort Walker:

In memory of
John M. Smith
Born September 9, 1842
Died at Hilton Head, South Carolina
June 3, 1865
It is not through age that here I lie.
So, friends, prepare yourselves to die.
Repent in time, make no delay.
I in my youth was called away.
Erected by his fellow workmen
CARPENTERS
Of the Quartermaster Department

At several places on the island there are Negro graveyards, with both slaves and freedmen and their freeborn descendants buried according to Negro tradition. The cups and plates used in the last illness, the glass pitchers, medicine bottles and spoons, or the lamps that kept sickbed vigil are decorating the graves or embedded in the headstones. Those who drowned at sea are always buried at the marsh edge, where high-tide waters will cover the graves, since the old superstition rules that the sea must receive again its own dead or claim a new victim.

A quick scanning of the dates in the cemetery beside Broad Creek shows that the first burial there was that of Lydia Page Davant, wife of James Davant, in 1795. This was seven years after the church was built there in 1788, and named "Zion Chapel of Ease." It came under the administraton of the pastor of the new St. Luke's Episcopal Church recently built on the mainland along Euhaw Road between Coosawhatchie and Screven's Ferry. St. Luke's was rebuilt half a mile north of the first site in 1824 on what is now Route 170, about three miles north of the junction with Route 46, and still later was sold to the Methodists, who still worship there. However, even though the new St. Luke's was closer than St. Helena's in Beaufort, it still was not close enough to Hilton Head for regular church attendance, and consequently funds were contributed for Zion Chapel to be built on the island itself.

The Stoneys of Fairfeld Plantation were among the chief contributors, and so were the Fripps. The building was neatly made of wood on a brick foundation, about forty by thirty feet in size. There was no parsonage, and when the minister came from St. Luke's on alternate Sundays, as he usually did, he spent the night at one of the island plantatons as welcome guest. Apparently some of the clergymen later bought land on the island, or had it given to them. One of the earliest pastors was the Reverend Andrew Mc-Cullough or McCully.

Next to the church along the public road, and possibly of earlier construction, was the muster house where militiamen met to drill. Some sort of requirements for landholders to furnish militia troops had been in force since early colonial days, and of course militia men had seen active service in the Revolution. With muster house, church and graveyard all located at the headwaters of Broad Creek, that bend in the road was surely a well-known island meeting place. Still a fourth factor was the Masonic Lodge, built just beyond the muster house. Masonry had been a part of Carolina life since the organization of the Solomon Lodge Number One in Charleston in 1735, and a Scottish Rite group would be organized at the turn of the century. William Drayton was Grand Master of the Fraternal Order of South Carolina Ancient York Masons when he died in 1790. Other familes on the island must have been members also, and although it seems surprising to find a lodge building in such a small and scattered community, evidently islanders used and enjoyed it.

A few other names must be added before the roster of the eighteenth century is completed. Two families, the Currels (Curls) and the Fylers, were neighbors of the Talbirds along Skull Creek, and the name "Currel's Sink" is still given to a swampy curve of the shoreline. Neighbors of the Davants on the south end were the families of Sara Waight, Thomas Ferguson and Dr. George Mosse. Elizabeth Mosse married her neighbor James Stoney at St. Helena's church on February 27, 1793. Their daughter Martha married Thomas Henry Barksdale, son of neighbors George and his second wife, Ann Agnes Bona. Thomas Henry was both born and buried on Hilton Head, and he left his estate to his wife, who also inherited land from her father. The land passed in turn to her second husband, Joseph Lawton, and to their son Samuel. In time the plantation became referred to simply as "Lawton's". Near neighbors on the north were William Fickling and his brother Samuel, the husband of Elizabeth Davant. Samuel and Elizabeth had three children: Jeremiah, William and Mary Ann. Another Davant sister, Lydia, married Thomas Webb of Marshlands, a plantation near the church.

In 1789 a widely-known planter, John Hanahan of Edisto, began acquiring land on Hilton Head, although he did not give up his Edisto property. He began with the purchase of 445 acres in the middle of the south shore, between Broad Creek and the Atlantic, and soon added 403 acres adjacent to the northeast, the land of the late Benjamin Guerard. In 1792 he added 270 acres between Crooked (Jarvis) Creek and Muddy Creek. This divided plantation soon became known as "Honey Horn" by the simple process of misspelling and mispronouncing plain Hanahan.

Also from Edisto were Thomas and William Eddings Baynard who added Braddock's Point, Spanish Wells and Muddy Creek Place to extensive holdings on the mainland. There was evidently an old house—old even in 1790— along Muddy Creek, for the stream was often called Old House Creek.

But the most important event that happened on Hilton Head in these years was the coming of William Elliott to Point Place, the old Barnwell grant, which he named "Myrtle Bank" in token of the green-leafed shrub that covered its seabrink slopes. Here in 1790 he raised what is generally acknowledged as the first successful crop of the long-staple cotton that would soon make the sea islands famous all over the world. Sea island cotton—and the wealth that went with it—opened a new era, a new way of living for the whole coastal area from St. John's Parish and the Santee River in Carolina to the Florida Everglades.

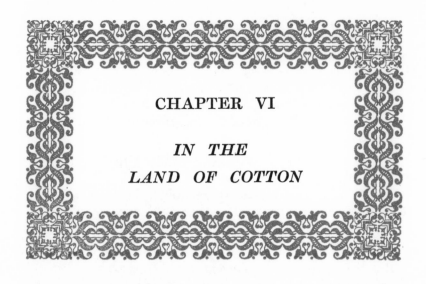

CHAPTER VI

IN THE
LAND OF COTTON

W ILLIAM ELLIOTT descended from a Bermuda
family whose sons came to the Carolinas about
1685. The Elliotts all had large families and
were "related in every direction"—as a family letter expressed it. There were William and Stephen Elliotts in
practically every generation, and the cotton-growing Elliott
of Hilton Head was the William who married Phoebe
Waight in 1787.

Of their seven children, daughter Phoebe Caroline would
marry Charles C. Pinckney of Pinckney Island "next door"
and son William would distinguish himself by writing of
Carolina sports. Among other Elliotts were clergymen, soldiers, a famous botanist, but for Hilton Head the Elliott
experiments with cotton were more important.

Seed for a long-staple cotton had already been imported
from the island of Anguilla in the Caribbean by both Georgia and Carolina planters. Some of the plantings grew
better than others. For William Elliott's first crop at
Myrtle Bank he had bought 5½ bushels of seed in
Charleston at 14 shillings a bushel, and he sold a large
yield of long, silky-fibered cotton at 10½ pence a pound.
Other planters began doing well with it, also, and one
named Kinsey Burden in Colleton County seemed to be
raising crops of uniform excellence. Burden never hinted

at the secret of his repeated success, but William Elliott was among the first to figure out for himself that the key to uniformly fine cotton year after year was a very, very careful selection of seed. Only the best seed from the best pods on the best plants were to be saved for the next crop. He told his theory of seed selection to all who would listen, and all who followed the practice soon prospered. By 1799 sea-island cotton fetched 5 shillings a pound in Liverpool, and the price would go still higher. In 1828 Hugh Wilson sold two bags of the best sea-island cotton for two dollars a pound. No wonder men said that cotton was king of the south!

Now Hilton Head land began to sell at prices as fancy as its cotton, and small planters were bought out by more ambitious ones until the island's thirty thousand acres were divided among fifteen or sixteen families who would keep their holdings till wartime confiscation. By mid-century the principal landholders were these: Baynards, Chaplins, Draytons, Elliotts, Ficklings, Gardners, Grahams, Jenkinses, Kirks, Lawtons, Mathews, Popes, Seabrooks, Scotts, Stoneys and Stuarts. The exact boundaries of their plantations are disputable since the official land records have been twice burned. Furthermore, ownership surely changed more than once during the sixty years of cotton's reign, to allow for dower settlements on young daughters and the claims of more than one son. Also, the census record for these years is listed only for the parish as a whole and definite residence on Hilton Head cannot always be ascertained, even from this source. However, the plantation names and boundaries can at least be approximated with reasonable accuracy and are so shown on the map that follows.

The standard map for this period is that drawn by C. Vignoles and R. Ravenel from surveys made in 1820. It was copied, with some changes, by Robert Mills for his widely accepted *Statistical Atlas of South Carolina*, printed in 1825. The Mills atlas notes three holdings of the Pope family, and other familiar names also appear. Two new labels are Park's Creek, for the former Bear Creek, and the addition of the name "Old Woman Folly" near the

Lawton property. Sometimes this was copied "Old Woman's Folly" as if to mark the spot of some elderly female foolishness. More likely, folly has the old English meaning: amidst woods; a clump of trees, especially fir trees. A folly was also an English public pleasure garden or a French vacation house. Farther to the north, near the headwaters of Fish Creek, other maps give "Folly Marsh" or "Folly Field." This latter was also called "Mathew's Folly Field" and then simply "Mathew's." The later owner was the Reverend Philip Mathews, husband of Rebecca Davant, and the minister at Zion Chapel.

In addition to William Elliott, Hilton Head was fortunate in having another planter who knew a great deal about growing sea-island cotton, William Seabrook. Seabrook was next neighbor to the Elliotts, for he bought the four plantations formerly owned by Talbird, Currel, Fyler and Wallis. He was among the first to advocate using salt-marsh muck as fertilizer for the cotton fields. Using marsh muck one year and ground oyster shells the next became fairly standard practice here and elsewhere in the sea islands, and the crop yields were tremendous.

Cotton was the main crop, of course, but it was not the only one. Some indigo was still raised on Hilton Head and some rice, although only where there was no threat of flooding by the sea, since salt water ruined the rice seedlings. Fields of corn and sugar cane were planted for family use, and there were gardens for both the "Big House" and the slave cabins. Each fall mounds of potatoes— meaning *sweet* potatoes, of course— were buried in the yard to last the winter through, and often there was a small patch of benne seed to harvest, for benne seed cookies and brittle candy were favorites all along the Carolina coast and have been ever since the Lords Proprietors had recommended their planting for the extraction of sesame oil.

There was little farm machinery, and even oxen were seldom used for plowing. The hard work of grubbing out the weeds in the cotton rows was done by a black hand on an old fashioned hoe. Slave women and children did most of the cotton picking, and seventy-five pounds a day was considered good work, while a hundred pounds was worthy of praise. The cotton bolls did not open as wide as short staple types and so picking was more difficult here than in mainland fields.

The cotton fields were laid out into squares about a fourth of an acre in size, or 105 feet. This amount of land was the basic unit of work and was called a "task," a word still used today by island farmers. Before 1820 the cotton was shipped off just as the pickers brought it to the shed, mixed with dead leaves and luncheon scraps, corn husks, and maybe a stray acorn or string. But presently Elliott and Seabrook and some of the other planters realized that if they were going to command the highest prices for a quality crop, they had to ship clean fiber. Consequently they began dividing the sheds into separate rooms for each step of the cleaning process and insisting on painstaking care. The result was increased profit and a higher credit balance on the account books of the factor or agent who sold the crops in Charleston or Savannah.

These were money-making years on Hilton Head, only slightly interrupted by wartime. On August 22, 1813, the British landed in force on Hilton Head shores and repeated their plunderings of Revolutionary War days. The island was defenseless, with no fortifications, and its homes too widely scattered to unite against sudden attack. Once again homes were burned and looted, and no doubt the Talbird house burning and the murder of Charles Davant were told again in bitterness.

The Mexican War of 1848 also broke into the peaceful tranquility of island ways and several island families sent their sons to serve along the border. Among these was young Lieutenant James Stuart, whose family had bought Otter Hole from John Stoney, and letters from the front boasted that he was the first over the walls at the capture of Mexico City. Alas, he escaped the storm of Mexican bullets only to meet death by Indian arrow years later in the wild west.

When war days were over, Hilton Head boys went off

to college in the North or in England, took the Grand Tour
of Europe and came home to read their books and pursue
their favorite hobbies of hunting and fishing. Their sisters
went traveling also, and bought gowns in Paris, bonnets in
London, musical instruments in Italy and frills and trinkets
wherever fancy took them. Some of the travelers made
more serious purchases. Two beautiful silver chalices made
by the Barnard silversmiths in Paternoster Row, London,
were brought to Hilton Head in 1834 for use in the Zion
Chapel communion service and were greatly treasured, although worship might be held there only five or six times
a year, for want of a pastor. No doubt those graceful chalices were part of the re-consecration of the chapel after
some years of disuse, for church records of 1829 reported
that the chapel had been "thrown out of use as to the worship for which it had been originally erected." Small wonder that the church was little used, since the minister in
charge of St. Luke's Parish was supposed—for an annual
salary of $700—to hold services not only at St. Luke's
and Zion Chapel, but also in the courthouse at Coosawhatchie and in the Union Chapel at Grahamville.

Among the pastors who served at Hilton Head were the
Reverend Andrew McCullough (McCully), Philip Ma-
thews, Samuel Sitgreaves (1821), Peter Van Pelt (1824),
Thomas J. Young (1827), B. C. Webb (1836-38), Alsop
Woodward (1839-53), James Stoney (1853-61). Serving
as assistants were J. B. Seabrook and the Reverend J. W.
Taylor and a layworker, C. R. Cross. These last three did
special missionary work among the Negroes. The Reverend
Philip Mathews served at intervals and seemed to have
Zion Chapel in his special charge for some years. This was
no doubt due to his residence here and his marriage to Rebecca Davant. For some time the couple lived at Sandhill
Plantation and also managed the five hundred acres known
as Folly Field, a short distance away. Other ministers occasionally officiated at Zion Chapel, however. When John
Loyer Davant married Mary Bourquin there in 1830, the
clergyman was the Reverend Joseph Wallace. On Monday, February 1, 1841, when Miss Eliza Pope, daughter

of William and Sarah Pope, married Alsop Woodward, rector of St. Luke's, the service was read by the Reverend Mr. Neufville of Christ Church, Savannah.

After 1831 the rector of St. Luke's was also called on to serve his parishioners at the new summer resort town of Bluffton on May River, just across from Hilton Head. The town was first called "Kirk's Bluff" or "Pope's Bluff" since so many of these two families lived there, but after some rivalry the family names were dropped. William Pope gave land for the Bluffton church in 1842, and the building was dedicated as Chapel of the Cross. A new larger building was erected in 1857 and is still standing. The building committee included Thomas Drayton, J. J. Pope, G. Henry Guerard, and William J. Graham. No doubt other oldtime families from Hilton Head worshipped there when they were on the mainland, and present island residents entering here have the right to imagine rustling crinolines, lacy shawls, beribboned bonnets and tall beaver hats of long bygone years. In time, of course, the Chapel of the Cross had its own clergyman, and since many islanders also had homes near Bluffton, there were usually folk from Hilton Head in the congregation.

Because most of the Hilton Head planters also owned land elsewhere, the real family home was often in Beaufort or Charleston. The Elliott family home, called "The Anchorage", and the Stuart home, later the Sea Island Hotel, stood side by side on Beaufort's Bay street facing the water. With these town houses to maintain in luxury, the island "Big Houses" were not the pillared mansions one expects to find in the wealthy Carolina Low Country. Many of the houses were more country places, ample and airy, but not elaborate. When the family moved out from the town house to the island, it was a simple matter to load the boat with fine silver and linen, with crystal goblets carefully packed, with the new musical instruments lately bought in Italy and anything else that might be wanted to make life pleasant and comfortable.

The Davant plantation house at Point Comfort, for example, was described in 1823 as a "tolerable comfortable dwelling house with kitchen and other buildings." Davant grandchildren remembered it as a big two-story house with a wide piazza where Grandfather Davant used to read Sunday service from the Episcopal prayer book to the accompanying music of waves washing the shore.

Charles Pinckney looked back on his Grandmother Elliott's house at Myrtle Bank and remembered it like this:

"I recall an oldfashioned country home on the riverbank, when the shades of evening and the breath of spring lured the family to the piazza. The harp in hands of a skillful musician, accompanied by her brothers on flute and clarinet, imprinted sweet sounds on the memory . . . Down the broad avenue over-arched by the patriarchal live oaks and verdant magnolia, you saw the moonbeams dancing on the waters of Port Royal, the peerless river of our southern coast, while the orange trees and the jasmine embowering the piazza and clamberng up its posts perfumed the air with odors sweet . . . The Negroes' keen ear for music would draw them from their homes. Seated on the grass around the house, they counted it a privilege to hear Miss Mary's harp . . ."

Young Stephen and William Elliott remembered less of the jasmine-scented air and more of the wonderful fishing on Hilton Head, the excitement of boat racing and the keen rivalry between plantations over the speed of the Negro oarsmen dressed in jaunty livery. Young Stephen was one for going out in his own sailboat, come high wind or good weather, and his grandmother was sure he was going to be drowned.

"Oh, no, ma'am," he assured her one day, according to family legend, and there was a roguish twinkle in his eye as he said it. "A boat is meant to keep you from being drowned. I promise you I'll never be drowned while there's a boat between me and the water."

"Humph!" said Mistress Elliott. "And if your boat is upset, what then?"

"I'll climb up and sit on the bottom," he replied promptly. "I've been there before, ma'am. It's a good place to be."

William thought his grandfather's tales of chasing the giant devil fish were the best stories ever told. His own forays after this horned, batlike sea monster were worth the telling also. He sent his article about this "Fishing Extra-ordinary" to the *American Turf Register* and *Sporting Magazine*, which promptly published it. Later the article was copied by the New England *Galaxy* and Boston*Mercury* (Dec. 25, 1829) and other newspapers. Eventually he included this first account with others in his book, *Carolina Sports By Land and Water*.

The method of catchng this huge winged fish—measuring twenty feet or more across the back—was to spear it with a harpoon fastened to the prow of a boat with a heavy rope. Once the fish felt the barb pierce its flesh, it would dash up the channel at great speed, while on the other end of the rope came the boat, willy-nilly, skimming the water as if on wings itself. At last exhaustion would send the great fish floundering to the beach, and the fishermen could claim their trophy.

Once, so Grandfather Elliott related, the fish had shown such endurance that there was time for him to call out to watching slaves on the bank and order a bowl of arrack punch to quench the thirst raised by the fantastic voyage. The punch was prepared quickly, brought to the end of the dock and passed down to him as the boat swept by. Very good punch it was, too, Grandfather always added, refreshing and exhilarating, as arrack punch should be.

Evidently the devilfish disappeared from Port Royal Sound some years after that epic, and the saga of the monster-chasing adventures of Grandfather Elliott had been largely forgotten when one summer day the fish re-appeared, furnishing William with material for another story:

"A respectable planter named Jones* who was remarkable for his mechanical ingenuity was in the habit of amusing himself during the long summer solstice in

*Probably not the real name, as Elliott customarily used only initials or fictitious names.

constructing curious, self-invented pieces of mechanism. Like a thousand others, he attempted to discover perpetual motion.

"It so happened that while Jones was engaged in these queries he had gone to Beaufort in a small boat manned with but two oars, and met on his return to his plantation, which lay near the sea, two devilfish disporting themselves on the surface of the water as innocently as if they had been angel fish; now showing the dark hues of their broad back, now thrusting up a horn, now vibrating a wing, and now impelling their enormous mass high in the air by the level of their powerful wings.

"Jones was a sportsman to the backbone. He cast a glance at the smallness of his boat, but it was a glance only; his eye rested on the bright harpoon which lay invitingly at his side. He sprang forward, secured his line to the head of the boat and darted his harpoon at the nearest sportive monster. A violent fall at full length into the bottom of the boat as it shot forward, almost from beneath his feet, was the first indication he received that his aim had been good. Casting up his eyes he beheld his little boat buried, as it were, in the waters, while the divided waves curved over it, but fell not, such was the rapidity of its motion, till they were well astern.

"His oarsmen, like prudent fellows, had taken through choice the prone position which the master had adopted through necessity, and quietly prostrated themselves in the bottom of the boat where they rightly supposed their situation was safest . . .

"It was not till some minutes had elapsed that he had the presence of mind, or the power, to crawl from his recumbent position to occupy his appropriate seat at the stern, where, however, he soon settled himself and enjoyed the whole luxury of his situation. The wind fanned his face. His hair streamed off at right angles from his head. The waters foamed furiously about the stern. And the boat, impelled by this more back to Fortress Monroe. The four lost transports were the *Peerless*, which sank after colliding with the *Star of the South*, sent to her assistance, and whose crew was saved by the gunboat *Mohican*; the *Osceola* and the *Union*, both of which went ashore, and had all on board made prisoners; and the *Governor*, whose 350 marines, under Major John George Reynolds, with the exception of a corporal and six men, were saved by the frigate *Sabine*, Captain Ringgold, which happened to be within view of its signs of distress.

The sealed orders which had been given each vessel of the expedition directed its rendezvous off Port Royal bar, where the *Wabash* and many others anchored on the morning of November 4th.

Additional arrivals followed in time. Soundings were made under the united direction of Mr. Boutelle, of the Coast Survey, and of Commander Charles H. Davis, fleet captain and chief of the commodore's staff, and on the 5th of November a reconnoissance of the Confederate works was made in force by Commander John Rodgers, of the *Flag*, and by General Wright, with the

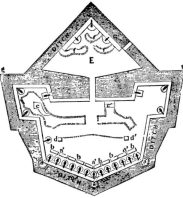

PLAN OF FORT WALKER.

gunboats *Curlew*, *I. P. Smith*, *Ottawa* and *Seneca*.

These had not proceeded far up the channel when they were met by four Confederate steamers, with which a lively exchange of fire soon took place, they retreating as the Federal gunboats advanced toward the batteries on Hilton Head and at Bay Point opposite.

When within range, the batteries opened on the Federals, as was naturally expected, and another engagement of nearly an hour ensued, when the object of the reconnoissance having been accomplished, the gunboats hauled off.

It was decided to attack the forts the following day, but a high wind having come up, this was found impossible, and it was not until the 7th November, 1861. that it could be properly made. The forced delay in commencing operations had enabled the Confederates to strengthen their defenses. Earthworks had been put up wherever practicable.

The largest of all, named Fort Walker, stood on Hilton Head, contained twenty-four guns, and was commanded by General T. F. Drayton, the brother of Captain Percival Drayton,

Burial place of those killed at HiltonHead

The Soldier In Our Civil War — Compiled from *Frank Leslie's Illustrated News Magazine*

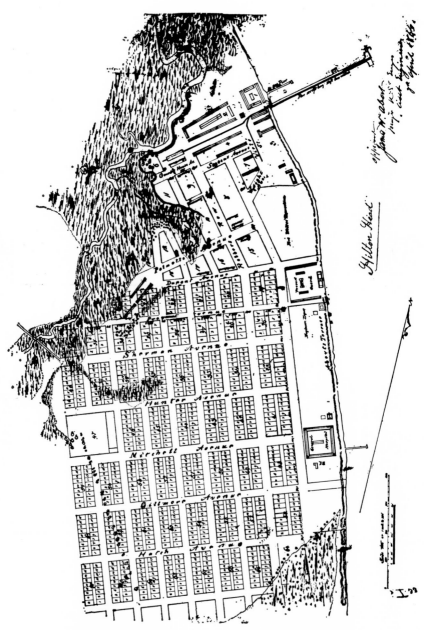

U.S. Tax Commission Map of City of Hilton Head and
the Fort, April, 1864 — *National Archives*

than Triton, darted through the waters with the speed of an arrow.

"Now he approached his home and rejoiced to see that several of his friends were assembled on the bluff to welcome his return. But what was their amazement to behold and recognize Jones seated upright in the stern of his boat which seemed to fly through the water without the aid of oar, oarsman, sail or steam or any apparent or visible impulsion! Amazement was their first emotion—joy was their second—and they suddenly shouted with triumph as the thought flashed upon them: 'JONES HAS DISCOVERED PERPETUAL MOTION!'

"He shouted to them for assistance, 'Man a boat! Rescue me!' His voice was tremulous with excitement and drowned by distance and never reached their ears. He waved his hat and shouted again. Hats waved in return and a triumphant shout came from his friends, but no boat put off, no rescue came . . .

The fish did pause at last, but not until the boat had been hurried quite out of the harbor and was floating on the broad waters of the Atlantic. It was then our sportsman cut off with his penknife the line which bound him to his formidable companion. The oars had been lost overboard in the melee, but fortunately the sail remained to waft him home . . . late at night . . . exhausted by excitement and fatigue . . . and he explained to his anxious friends the mystery of his unintelligible , but—fortunately for him—not *perpetual* motion."

For less adventuresome souls the oyster roast furnished a happier pastime, especially during the Christmas holidays or at New Year's. Friends would be invited from other islands roundabout and they would come riding to the party in their barges instead of the carriages they would have used in Beaufort. More than once there was good-natured racing to see which boatload of guests would be first at the dock, and there was keen rivalry between well-matched crews. Once ashore, there was gracious welcome, friendly laughter. Carts had been carrying supplies to the picnic beach since sunrise, and the oysters were ready in the barrels of salt water that kept them fresh. Oak and hickory logs made the fire hot and cedar boughs gave it fragrance. The table was spread with plain linen mats, and a special oyster knife with a guarded handle was laid at each place. When everyone was ready, the steaming oysters were brought on wooden plates and all fell to the messy business of eating with a fervor and gaiety no doubt heightened by hot whisky punch. Other menus might be served with ancestral silver, imported cloths, lovely crystal-ware, but it was not island custom to curtail the full enjoy-ment of juicy oysters with such dainty accessories.

Hunting was always a favorite island pastime. Although a slave was usually delegated with responsibility for bring-ing duck, quail and marsh hen for the "Big House" table, his duties must have been light when there were men and boys in the family. It is said that William Elliott had the custom of displaying his bag of birds on a silver platter which the butler carried to the drawing room for the ladies to ad-mire both the plumage and the prowess. Some of the older men began to grumble that there wasn't as much game as in the old days—too many people.

The growing number of residents on Hilton Head in these years is evidenced by the appointment of the first post-master on Feb. 16, 1858. William E. Pope, Jr., was named and he served until the office was discontinued on October 6, 1859. No doubt the post office was on his property, de-scribed as bounding Fish Haul on the north. It was pos-sibly an extension of the family plantation, "Cotton Hope," or may be the Piney Woods tract. The mailboat usually docked at Seabrook's wharf. Fenn Peck of Charleston was was given the contract to carry the mail between that city and Savannah, and postal records show he made thirteen round trips a quarter for the price of $25 each trip. His boat left Charleston each Friday morning at seven, stopped at Beaufort, Boyd's Landing and Bluffton as well as Hil-ton Head, and was in Savannah by three o'clock the follow-ing afternoon, barring stormy weather. The return trip cleared Savannah docks by eight-thirty on Sunday night and tied up at Charleston again around five o'clock Tuesday afternoon. There were proposals for tri-weekly and even daily service by mail boat, but evidently these never materialized.

Additional letters for Hilton Head might be added to the mail sack at Bluffton, for mail addressed there could come as far as Hardeeville by train and then be carried the rest of the way by mule. Dr. J. H. Mellinchamp, the famous botanist and husband of Sarah Eilzabeth Pope, quipped to his correspondents that he answered their letters by return *mule.* His letters, however they were carried, brought Bluffton to the attention of students of science, and many have journeyed to see Mellinchamp's grave in St. Luke's churchyard.

Probably the discontinuance of the post office on Hilton Head in 1859 caused little inconvenience. There were always boats from one plantation or another going to the mainland, and everyone was always ready to carry a message for a neighbor. Possibly the office was discontinued at Mr. Pope's death, but the reason is not recorded. At any rate, Hilton Head returned to its former isolation bounded by winds, waves and weather.

On the sea islands, "weather" meant hurricanes. When late summer skies darkened and high waves lashed the beach fronts, both master and slave cocked a knowing eye at the heavens and remembered the old rhyme brought from the West Indies:

> June, too soon.
> July, stand by.
> August, come it must
> September, remember.
> October, all over.

One September hurricane that many remembered was the one that blew in on September 15, 1824, and others recalled the September winds of 1854, thirty years later. Old-timers harked back to 1804 when most of the sea islands were under water. Those were the years when a planter could see his whole twelve months' work ruined by just twelve hours of lashing wind and rain. Instead of having ninety thousand dollars or more to their credit on the books of the factor in Charleston, there would be a blank, or even a debit.

Other years left equally unpleasant memories with their record of devastation from insects and blight. Planters of sea-island cotton did not find life all worry-free profit, gay parties, leisure and sport.

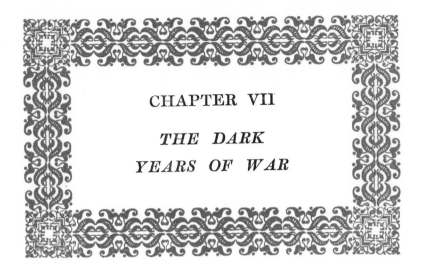

CHAPTER VII

*THE DARK
YEARS OF WAR*

BLACKER than any September hurricane sky were the war clouds of April, 1861. South Carolina had seceded the previous December, the first state to do so, and signing the Ordinance of Secession for Beaufort District was Richard James Davant, who had been born on Hilton Head in 1805. Others from the island were present when the first shot of the war was fired at Fort Sumter in Charleston Harbor on April 12.

The hatred and bitterness of those war years should surely be put aside by a nation once more united under one flag, but their heroism, gallantry and courage can be remembered with honor by both North and South. Hilton Head shares that honor, for the largest naval engagement ever fought in American waters took place off her shores when the war was scarcely six months old. As further distinction it was also the first full-scale landing by an American armed force on any fortified enemy shore; the first amphibious assault of combined Army and Navy strength operating together. It very narrowly missed a third distinction, that of being the first three-way attack by air, land and sea. An observation balloon for the expedition had been ordered by General McClellan from the civilian aeronaut, Professor T. S. C. Loewe, but it did not arrive in time to make any pre-battle observations. Nevertheless, the balloon was put

to use here in January 1862, manned by John B. Stark-
weather of Boston, and so Hilton Head deserves a place
in history as the site of the first triple-threat task force.

In the annals of the Confederacy, the battle for Hilton
Head had no such majestic aspect. It was merely a des-
perate, gallant attempt to do the impossible.

General P. G. T. Beauregard, commanding provisional
forces for the State of South Carolina, began mapping out
plans for coastal defense when the guns first opened the
war at Fort Sumter. Hilton Head, he reported to the governor, was one of the places that could and should be fortified, but strengthening the defenses of Charleston Harbor
came first. A month later he found time to examine the
entire coastline from Charleston to Savannah and reported
May 16:

> "I am of the opinion that the entrance to the mag-
> nificent and important harbor of Port Royal can be
> effectually protected by two strong works on Hilton
> Head and Bay Point, on each side of the entrance, and
> a steel-clad, floating battery moored half way between
> the two, all armed with the heaviest rifled guns that can
> be made, but the construction not being practicable at
> present, I have resorted to local works . . ."

Accompanying Beauregard on this inspection survey were
Lt. Col. George Elliott and the Cuban patriot, General
Ambrosio José Gonzales (who would marry Harriott Elliott of Hilton Head) and also Captain Francis D. Lee of
the Engineer Corps. The latter was assigned the task of
constructing the batteries. All of these men knew that the
heavy guns recommended by Beauregard were imperative
—and all of them knew that the Confederacy did not have
such weapons. Beauregard repeated his request. The ordnance officer repeated that they were not available.

Then re-assignment sent Beauregard on to become the
hero of Manassas, and young Francis Lee and his engineers
were left to do the best they could.

The battery on Hilton Head, located near the bluff headland that gave the island its name, was christened Fort Wal-

ker. No doubt the name was in honor of the Confederate Secretary of War, L. P. Walker with perhaps the hope that the Secretary would somehow find the heavy artillery needed for his namesake battlements. Perhaps, also, there was some idea of honoring W. S. Walker, then in charge of the third military district, of which Hilton Head was a part. Across the harbor mouth at Bay Point, Fort Beauregard was being built at the same time.

Work began in July, with the island planters furnishing the slave labor for hauling palmetto logs, digging trenches, erecting a powder magazine, constructing gun emplacements. The slaves sang as they worked. Nothing new about that. Slaves were always singing. The rhythm helped them work faster. But now as they sang they slurred the words whenever a white man was near, for this lilting, light-hearted tune told of the coming freedom, the freedom being brought by thousands of men in Yankee blue going to war:

"No more peck of corn for me, no more, no more.
No more peck of corn for me.
Many thousands go."

"No more pint of salt," the verses followed, naming another slave ration doled out each season. "No more driver's lash! No more mistress' call!" The song would spread through all the southland and no one knows its composer, but William Francis Allen and Lt. Col. John Trowbridge, both authorities on slave songs, believe that it was first sung on Hilton Head and Bay Point in that dark summer of 1861 while the slaves labored at Forts Walker and Beauregard.

The work went on, with or without the mumbled singing, and Major Francis D. Lee reported:

"The armament of the waterfront, as laid out by General Beauregard, consisted of 7 ten-inch Columbiads, and my plans were arranged for such a battery. The interior slopes of the water battery were consequently intended for seven circular transverses against enfilading fire.

The labor having arrived, the work was rapidly pressed forward, and by September 1, 1861 the fort was ready to receive its armament. In place of receiving 7 ten-inch guns, but one could be procured, together with 1 ten-inch Columbiad bored to a 24-pounder and rifled, 1 eight-inch Columbiad, 9 Navy 32-pounders . . ."

He went on to list a few smaller guns, but no more of the heavy-caliber weapons that Beauregard had said were essential. And there was no mention of the floating battery. In place of the heavy guns for beach defense, Lee received only two light carronades without carriages or chassis. His emplacements did not fit the smaller weapons, of course, and so their maneuverability was consequently limited still further.

At least the powder magazine was well built. He could be proud of that. But only part of the furnace for heating shot arrived. Somehow, under the direction of a Mr. Patterson, the men did manage to construct a makeshift furnace for the deadly hot-shot. Another crew was ordered to dig earthworks for the infantry about two miles to the south, and Lee also planned defenses at Braddock's Point and another battery on Skull Creek near Seabrook's Landing. Time was short and none of these projects was completed to his satisfaction. The Skull Creek defense was scarcely begun.

Word began filtering through to Confederate headquarters that the North was assembling a huge expeditionary fleet to attack Charleston and points south. A Confederate spy near Norfolk had picked up a Yankee hat with a Boston newspaper wadded into the crown. That newspaper gave alarming details of the fleet's size. Another spy sent word he had counted one hundred sailing ships in Hampton Roads. When Brigadier General Thomas Fenwick Drayton arrived at Beaufort on October 17, he learned that there were 362 men to defend Fort Walker against this assembling invasion. Drayton asked for re-inforcements and the new total was 622. With the new forces under Major Samuel Jones of the 12th South Carolina Volunteers, Drayton be-

LANDING OF UNITED STATES TROOPS AT FORT WALKER, AFTER THE BOMBARDMENT, NOVEMBER 7TH, 1861.

Leslie's News Magazine

Nursery at Elliott's Plantation
S. C. Historical Society

THE POST-OFFICE AT HILTON HEAD, SOUTH CAROLINA.

LANDING STORES AT HILTON HEAD, SOUTH CAROLINA.

OUR PICKET AT GENERAL DRAYTON'S MANSION, HILTON HEAD, SOUTH CAROLINA.—SKETCHED BY OUR SPECIAL ARTIST.—[SEE PAGE 773.]

Harper's Weekly, November 30, 1861

gan repairing the wharf at Seabrook so that ammunition and supplies could be landed there. His headquarters were both the Pope house at Coggins Point and his own home on the north side of Fish Haul Creek, called Fish Hall. If anyone knew how to defend the island, he would. Thomas Drayton knew every road, every woodland trail; knew where the off-shore waters were deep enough for landing. But without the necessary guns . . .

In immediate charge of the fort was Colonel John A. Wagener and 220 men of the First Artillery, South Carolina Militia. Major A. M. Huger was in charge of the firing. Captain Josiah Bedon and Co. C. of the 9th (later 11th) South Carolina Volunteers manned the waterfront. Captains Werner and Harmes with A and B Companies of the Germany Artillery, and Captains Canaday and White of the Infantry brought the total manpower to 687, later to be increased to about 1450. Other Ninth Volunteers under Capain H. M. Stuart manned the guns at Braddock's Point, another officer who had known the island since childhood. Acting as Drayton's aides were young lieutenant J. E. Drayton and captains T. R. S. Elliott and Ephraim Baynard, all of island families, and Captain Paul Seabrook was another who had known the island well in peace time and now served in its defense. Drayton checked positions with his staff, named Col. William C. Heyward in command and returned to Beaufort where he sent messages to General Ripley at Coosawhatchie and General Lawton in Savannah asking for re-inforcements. But even if more troops came before Federal attack, Drayton must have known that the island had no chance.

Meanwhile there assembled in the waters off Hampton Roads the "most formidable squadron ever fitted out in American waters," as the Northern newspapers called it. Fifty ships-of-war plus transports for 15,000 troops were indeed worth that description. With Flag Officer (later Admiral) Samuel F. DuPont in command of the fleet and General Thomas W. Sherman (not William Tecumseh) in charge of the troops, the expedition sailed from Hampton Roads under sealed orders on October 29, 1861, destina-

tion unknown to all but the chief strategists. As the vessels
reached Cape Hatteras such a violent storm seized them
that the entire fleet was scattered. When the weather got
control of itself, sealed orders were opened to discover the
meeting place and the secret was out: Destination, Port
Royal. Now the men could call this great venture by its
right name, the Port Royal Expedition. One by one the
storm-scattered captains took their bearings and headed for
the rendezvous.

The captain of the sloop-of-war *Pocahontas* must have
repeated that destination with dry lips. He was Percival
Drayton of Fish Hall Plantation, Hilton Head, brother of
Thomas, the island's defending general. So it would be
brother against brother. The bitter phrase would be echoed
to unbearable meaning in the war years ahead, but surely
no man could say it of himself without feeling the numb-
ness and pain were his alone.

Percival Drayton had not made his decision without
counting the cost. No man, Navy trained, could have overlooked the importance of Hilton Head as a naval base for
blockading southern ports. No man, Carolina bred, could
have forgotten the hot loyalty that would send the rest of
his family rallying to their loved State. But Percival Drayton had taken an oath to defend the government of the
United States as an officer in the Navy and for him that
oath negated all other loyalties.

When the fatal shot opening the war was fired at Fort
Sumter, Captain Drayton had been stationed in the Navy
Yard at Philadelphia and he had promptly asked that his
status as a citizen of seceding South Carolina be struck from
Navy records. From that day on he wished to be listed
as a reisdent of Philadelphia. The South Carolina legisla-
ture retaliated by declaring him "infamous" and making him
an outlaw. Percival did not waver. He wrote a friend that
he was quite willing to give his own life to keep his country
united, and if the battle took the last of his kinsmen as well,
then so it would have to be. He was not afraid to face
the consequences of his decision.

In fact, Drayton was not afraid of anything. At least

that was the opinion of Admiral David Farragut when he
chose Percival to be fleet captain and commander of the
flagship *Hartford* in the famous battle of Mobile Bay
three years later. But now in November 1861 there was
pain, if no fear, knowing that his brother—his friends,
neighbors, schoolmates, too—would be waiting at Hilton
Head. Behind the fort where the guns of the *Pocahontas*
would be aimed, his brother Thomas would give the signal
for answering fire. Terse-lipped, Percival Drayton gave
the order to proceed. He had already decided where his
first loyalty lay.

On another Northern vessel young volunteer aide-de-
camp Stephen Weld wrote in his diary:

Saturday Nov. 2: . . . The fleet is all scattered and
but four are now in sight. Our sealed orders were
opened today. *Sunday, Nov. 3:* . . . We started at four
o'clock this morning and headed due west. Came in
sight of land about nine. I think it must have been
Tybee Island at the entrance of the Savannah River.
The pilot will not say where we are . . . Our ship was
the first one to get here . . . and now five are in sight.

. . . Nineteen vessels this afternoon . . . *Monday,
Nov. 4:* A beautiful calm day . . . about thirty of the
fleet are now anchored off Port Royal. Several of the
gunboats are engaged in sounding the channel . . .
We heard cannon firing and saw our gunboats firing at
what we supposed were rebel gunboats. I could not see
anything very distinctly . . .

The Confederate gunboats numbered only four: The
Savannah, flagship of Commander Josiah Tattnall, under
Captain J. N. Moffit and fleet captain R. L. Page; the
Resolute, Lt. J. Pembroke Jones; the *Sampson,* Lt. J. Ken-
nard; and the *Lady Davis,* Lt. John Rutledge, commanding. A few days earlier the *Lady Davis,* with Captain Stephen Elliott aboard, and a crew of twenty, managed to
capture a Yankee sailing vessel of 1200 tons and bring the
prize back to Beaufort. It was a daring feat, but without
mishap. Young Elliott was still keeping his promise never

to drown so long as a boat was between him and the water. Now he was not with the fleet, but in charge of his own Beaufort Volunteer Artillery at Fort Beauregard. Under Col. R. G. M. Dunovant and Capt. Elliott, Fort Beauregard swore to defend Port Royal as long as there was shot to fire.

Aboard one of the Northern troop ships, the correspondent for the New York *Herald* watched the gunboats and scribbled hasty notes:

Tuesday, Nov. 5: At twenty minutes before seven o'clock the first gun was fired from the rebel flagship *Everglade,* and in less than one minute afterward the *Lady Davis* let slip a shot at the ships. In five minutes the firing became quite lively on both sides, the gunboat *Ottawa* opening fire on our side. The following boats took part: *Ottawa, Pembina, Seneca, Curlew, Penguin, Isaac Smith;* the *Pawnee* coming in after the firing had well advanced. As we drew up toward the batteries, the one on Hilton Head opened up on us, this being the first positve knowledge that there were guns at this place. . . . As this was only a reconnaissance . . . the recall signal was hoisted . . . Just as we were hauling off, the *Pawnee* got into position and opened fire on Hilton Head batteries. Most of her shot fell short, but a rifled 68 pounder threw in a shell beautifully.

Beside the reporter, an artist for *Harper's Weekly* was busy with his sketch pad. The magazine would want pictures of the assembled fleet, the shoreline with Fort Walker's guns pointed seaward, signal flags wigwagging battle orders, bursting shells from the gunboats. The correspondent went on scribbling:

The rebels throw in shot around the *Pawnee* very fast, but all fall short. Rebel navy comes down to follow us. The *Curlew* fires a few rounds. The little *Mercury* runs in, shows them her stern and lets drive a shell from her 30 pounder which bursts close to the rebel camp. Thus ended the first regular Army reconnaissance in which the Navy did all the work and the Army did half the looking on.

The Federal Army would have to be content with "half the looking on." Most of the landing gear had been lost overboard in the storm off Hatteras, and the troops could not land. While Sherman fumed at his helplessness, the men on the transports suddenly realized they had grandstand seats for the coming battle.

To Commander Tattnall and his gallant little squadron, those transports anchored away from the protecting gunboats looked like sitting ducks. If only he could slip past the armed ships he could fire at will upon them. Tattnall was daring enough to conceive the plan, but the odds were too heavy against him. There were too many gunboats and too much room for them to maneuver. He had to content himself that he had at least made their task more difficult by removing the channel markers. While they sounded out the channel, the men on Fort Walker and Bay Point would gain a little more time.

The weather granted another full day of respite. On Wednesday, November 6, even the powerful Federal Navy was helpless under the driving of a strong westerly wind. Over on Hilton Head General Drayton re-organized his defense. It was obvious that there would be no attack at the island's southern tip and so he recalled Capt. Stuart at Braddock's Point and ordered him to cross the channel to support Elliott at Fort Beauregard. However, the steamer *Edith* did not come to transport them in the high wind, and the men did not leave till the following day. Meanwhile, in spite of wind and weather, reinforcements arrived. From Savannah Brigadier-General Alexander Lawton sent 450 men of the Georgia Infantry under Captain Berry plus Captain Read's battery of two twelve pound howitzers and fifty men. A little later Colonel W. D. De-Saussure and 650 men of the 15th South Carolina Volunteers landed at Seabrook wharf. At Camp Lookout on the beach about six miles from the fort were Capt. I. H. Screven's mounted guerillas ready to act as scouts and couriers. In the woods to the south of the fort Capt. Paul Seabrook and 25 men were posted on picket duty, and another picket was stationed under the high bluff to the north of Fish Haul Creek mouth.

The morning of the seventh came with clear sky and no wind. Out on the calm sea the Federal ships began forming into the egg-shaped battle line planned by Admiral DuPont. At his lookout post on the bluff Drayton sat astride his white horse watching. It did not take his trained soldier's eye long to grasp the deadliness of that slowly advancing line, each ship a vessel's length behind the other. So moving, they could bring their guns to bear first on Fort Beauregard, then deliver a broadside to swamp Tattnall's tiny fleet and turn seaward to fire at Hilton Head. They had only to keep moving, keep firing, there in the ample waters of Port Royal to reduce both forts to ruin. Drayton wheeled his horse aboutface and rode back to the fort. Dismounting, he tossed the reins to a wide-eyed pickaninny. "Take care of him. I'll be back. Hear?" he ordered, and the next moment was deep in plans for counter attack. He had 24 guns to at least 150 for the enemy, but those 24 would not be silent.

Across the calm water the line of ships came: the steam frigates *Wabash* and *Susquehanna*, sloops-of-war *Mohican*, *Seminole*, *Pawnee*. Gunboats *Pembina* and *Unadilla*. The sailing-sloop-of-war, *Vandalia*, towed by the *Isaac Smith* whose guns had been thrown overboard in the gale off Hatteras. One ship was missing, the *Union*, wrecked in that same gale, and captured and her sealed orders had been opened by the Confederates. Forming a flanking column were the gunboats *Bienville*, *Seneca*, *Penguin* and *Augusta*. On they sailed in majesty, while in the water off Joiner's Bank the transports rode at anchor and eager soldiers crowded to the rails to watch. Newspaper reporters and artists elbowed to a place beside them. It was just a little past nine o'clock. Boom! The opening shot from Fort Walker zoomed toward the *Wabash*, fell short.

The reporter from *Harper's Weekly* sent his pencil flying across his note pad:

"In three minutes another shot from the battery. Cheers from the transports, but no firing from our side as yet."

The *Wabash* was only waiting till she was in position, and now there was action enough. *Harper's* would tell it all in full detail in the issue of November 30:

In a few minutes the *Wabash* opened a smart fire, throwing her shells into the woods where the rebels were camped in some force. After firing a few guns to ascertain the range, she opened a broadside fire on both batteries, which was one of the finest sights ever witnessed in this country. Now the troops did cheer. It was both hearty and long. The other vessels now opened their fire, and the shells fell thick and fast into the battery. The rebels now opened a smart fire, and it was a subject of general remark at the fine shots they made. The small gunboats now steamed rapidly ahead and opened on them with ten and eleven inch pivot guns. At fifteen minutes past ten o'clock the fire was so hot that the Confederate gunboats uphelmed and started for Broad River, our gunboats chasing them. By this time the shells were bursting in the Bay Point Battery at the rate of about two a minute, to which the rebels replied with rapidity and great execuiton.

The flagship and her division were rapidly drawing to the point around which they would turn to come down along the shore and engage Hilton Head Battery, while the small gunboats took up independent positions and battered away at Bay Point and the rebel naval vessels. As the *Wabash* turned so that her broadside could bear upon the rebel fleet, she opened fire upon them and soon sent them upriver for a time, at least . . .

At about twenty minutes to eleven o'clock the *Wabash* commenced operations on the Hilton Head Battery in earnest . . . The noise was terrific, while the bursting of shells was as terrible as it was destructive. I counted no less than forty shells bursting at one time and that right in the woods where about 800 rebels lay. In addition to this, the *Susquehannah* with her tremendous battery, aided by the *Bienville*, the *Pawnee* and a half a dozen smaller gunboats, was making the air brown with sand, while the blue smoke of the explosions went to make up a most magnificent sight. The troops went wild with enthusiasm, and with deafening cheers they applauded the boldness and courage of the gallant naval officer. A moment or two had elapsed—just time enough to load the guns— and again the scene was enacted afresh. The rebels replied with seven guns which were working splendidly, and from appearances they did considerable execution . . .

At eleven o'clock they had reached as near to the reef as it was safe to go and they were obliged to haul off to again take up their positions, but giving another broadside as they turned . . . At half past eleven the *Wabash* and her consorts drew near the Hilton Head battery again, the rebels keeping up a brisk fire upon them as they approached . . . At ten minutes before twelve o'clock again the ships were enveloped in a dense cloud of white smoke, and in a few seconds shells were bursting into the battery in a splendid manner. The sand was flying in every direction and it seemed impossible that anyone who was within the walls of the battery could be saved from death. The rebels worked only two guns, I will give them the credit that they worked them beautifully. In just twenty minutes over two hundred shells burst over their heads and in the works . . . The rebel battery is badly damaged and the houses and tents bear the marks of shells . . . It looks as if there is a stampede in the rebel camp . . . The gunboats pepper away at the battery, which only replies with one gun . . . At two o'clock we weigh anchor and go still closer in, feeling assured they have become pretty well used up and will not—or cannot— injure us.

The phrase *cannot injure* was the correct one. The fort itself had been little damaged, only ten were killed and about twenty or so wounded, but the guns were useless. About twelve-thirty Drayton turned Fort Walker over to Colonel Heyward and withdrew to see if the reinforcements promised by General Ripley were arriving. About a mile from the fort he met Ripley and his staff, but no troops, although some of the requisitioned arms and food had been landed at Seabrook. Ripley returned to Coosawhatchie, hoping he could bring reinforcements soon enough, although this did not seem likely. Heyward, with instructions to hold the fort as long as effective fire could be returned, checked on ammunition supply. The answer from Lt. Scanlon at the magazine was not encouraging—only ten or eleven rounds for the 32 pounders remained. Heyward and Major Huger took the only recourse of firing two guns slowly so that the wounded could be evacuated first, then the rest of the defenders. In charge of those final guns were Capt. Bedon and Lieutenants J. E. Heape, J. J. Guerard and W. A. Boyle, and Heyward would recommend the four of them in his report for behaving with distinguished bravery. Two aides, Hugh Rose and Joseph Huger, were commended for rendering great assistance and displaying great coolness.

Meanwhile Drayton was commandeering all available boats and barges to aid in retreat to the mainland, and he sent his volunteer aide, Capt. T. R. S. Elliott, to examine the creeks beyond Bay Point. Young Tom Elliott was the man to send. He was as enthusiastic a fisherman as his father and had even taken part in devil-fishing, and he knew every inlet and marsh. If there was a back-door route from Bay Point to Beaufort, he would find it.

The reporter who had said that it looked like a stampede at Fort Walker was not far from right. No time for orderly retreat. The barges had to come and go with the tide and could not wait. No time for getting knapsacks and keepsakes. No time for eating the hot food steaming in the cook tents. Time only to rescue the battle flags—and run. The flag of South Carolina, the bonnie blue flag with its one bright star, was ripped and torn with shell fragments, but still intact. The battle flag of the Confederacy had taken shellfire fullface and not even a grayed ribbon of it could be found. In the plantation Big Houses, the women and children who had not already escaped bundled their treasures together—or buried them—and with a few house servants to help them crossed over to the mainland.

At Fort Beauregard Captain Stephen Elliott was wounded, but he kept up the firing as long as there was counterfire from the guns at Hilton Head. Col. Dunnovant was in command but he knew that the Elliotts were on home ground and he turned the retreat over to their charge. Young Thomas had picked out the route, Captain Stephen confirmed it and cousin Stephen, the chaplain, went ahead to negotiate for flat boats to ferry the men across deep water at two points. For the rest, the journey could be made on foot across the Narrows Path, a marshy trail known to few and passable by men walking single file. They made it, finally, crossing in the late afternoon, with the help of flatboats assembled, by a Beaufort Citizens' Committee of Thomas Hanckel, Henry Stuart and W. H. Cuthbert. They went on to make a stand beyond Beaufort at Camp Lee near Pocataligo, leaving Beaufort abandoned by both soldiers and citizenry.

The retreat from Hilton Head took longer, for there were more troops involved. Although the fort itself was emptied by two in the afternoon, there were still graycoated soldiers waiting at Ferry Point on Skull Creek till long after midnight. Others severely wounded did not get that far. There in the dark tangles of myrtle bushes matted together with jack vines and Cherokee roses they waited and wondered why the damnyanks didn't come butcher them where they lay and get it over with. No Yanks came. The retreat went on unmolested. Tattnall, who had scarcely stopped to breathe, took the last load across to Bluffton about one-thirty and then went on to Savannah by the inland waterway, carrying the troops from Georgia who wanted to go back home.

General Robert E. Lee, newly appointed commanding general of the area, was hastening to Port Royal with plans for its defense, but Forts Beauregard and Walker had

fallen to the enemy before he could reach them. General
Drayton's telegram announcing that he had retired to Bluffton was already on the way. Lee replied: "Find out enemy
intentions . . . defend New River Bridge . . . protect inland
water passes to Charleston . . . push cavalry as close to
enemy as prudent . . ." The word *prudent* did not leave
them much scope. The whole force along the coast from
Charleston to Savannah was less than four thousand men,
barely enough for a thin line of defense and surely not
sufficient for punishing attack. The next move was up to the
Yankees.

Meanwhile, on that wartorn afternoon of November 7,
the Federal transports launched a hundred or so surf boats,
ready to disembark troops. At half past two the *Wabash*
came down the channel past Fort Walker and fired one
gun. No answering fire. The forts were abandoned.
The *Harper's* correspondent wrote feverishly:

> Twenty minutes to three . . . whaleboat of the
> *Wabash* manned. White flag of truce flying over the
> bow and Commander John Rodgers in the stern.
> Starts for shore. Every stroke of oars watched by
> thousands of anxious eyes. She strikes the beach. Capt.
> Rodgers, borne on the back of true and trusty tars, with
> the Stars and Stripes floating over his head and a large
> ensign, goes ashore. At three o'clock precisely the
> Stars and Stripes wave in triumph over the South Caro-
> lina shore and the deserted rebel battery.

The young volunteer aide, Stephen Weld, suddenly
found that there was more to warfare than cheering wildly
from the safe deck of an anchored transport. He was now
on the staff of General Horatio Gates Wright and had
orders to report in uniform ready for duty. This he managed to do, with the help of a good deal of borrowed plumage, since he had embarked without uniforms and indeed
without official appointment, through family influence. By
half-past five he was stepping from the boat to Hilton
Head Beach and went up to the fort. There he found the
marines "jolly drunk on whisky," as he wrote in his diary,

and he helped his superior officers send the celebrating visitors back to their ships while military authorities took over.

While hurrying back from one of his many errands, Weld scuffed over an envelope with the figures $291.31 scrawled on the outside. Most of the sum had already been pilfered, but he did find one twenty-cent shinplaster and a ten-cent one, and later he added a dollar bill drawn on the bank of South Carolina to his trophies. He also acquired the wreath from a hat belonging to the Confederate surgeon Dr. Buist, whose body had been left in the fort.

Weld added page after page to his diary. This was something the folks at home would want to read about:

The scene on the beach where the soldiers were landing surpasses description. Guns going off, some fired by drunken marines and others by disorderly soldiers, men screaming, yelling, and rushing about in perfect disorder made altogether a perfect pandemonium of the place. It could hardly be avoided, though, due to the manner in which soldiers had landed: they being in small boats and easily scattered, it was a work of much difficulty getting them together again. Gen. Wright soon got his brigade together and immediately garrisoned the fort and stationed pickets and posted all the regiments, making them sleep on their arms, ready at a moment's notice. He took me with him at 2 a. m. and made the rounds. I got an hour's sleep at headquarters and was glad enough to get that. I was so busy most of the time I had no chance to get any plunder . . . Many of the marines got swords, pistols, guns, watches, etc. from the tents . . . the general was going around stopping the men from plundering . . . It was quite a pretty sight in the evening when the moon had gone down to see over a hundred fires burning in every direction and groups of soldiers around them talking, smoking and joking as if safe at home . . .

Friday, Nov. 8: I went back into the island and saw a dead rebel killed by one of our shells. I passed cotton fields, sugar cane and sweet potato fields in any quantity and finally came to a house about 2½ miles into the island where there were four rebels, three mortally and one severely wounded. One of them had just died under operation cutting his leg off and those horrible turkey buzzards, could be seen hovering in the air over the house, smelling even so soon the dead man. It was a horrible sight and made one feel what war was. I found a rebel knapsack which I took home with me. The road was strewn with them for two miles back.

Some days later he led twenty-five men on a foraging expedition, looking for corn or whatever could be found, and reported that the Seabrook home had already been plundered by Negroes and soldiers so that little remained. At Pope's Cotton Hope Plantation, which he thought the nicest on the island, it was the same story and he could find only a piece of clock as a memento. On Pinckney Island he appropriated a bale of cotton, the first of some half a million dollars worth sent to New York from the Sea Islands between November, 1861, and mid-June, 1862.

The men under brigadier-generals Wright, Stevens and Viele now pitched their tents near the Pope house at Coggins Point, which served as headquarters. Other troops were quartered in the other houses, especially those overlooking the waterways where Confederate landing parties might be expected. The Yankees did not have long to wait. As soon as possible small raiding bands of Confederates rowed across from Bluffton by night, set fire to the cotton baled for shipping North, set fire to the crops in the field and the houses themselves. In spite of Federal vigilance, the raids continued on all the islands up and down the coast, and Stephen Elliott was credited with having destroyed fourteen plantation homes in a single night. Elliott also did major work in developing a sunken torpedo for blasting ships. Now the raiding parties came by daylight, doing their best to tempt the large Yankee ships into Skull Creek where several of the torpedoes had been planted.

On December 6, a raiding party was led by the Kirk

brothers, John and Rollin, and there were numerous others reported in the Official Records, including the Skull Creek Affair and the Pope's (Jenkins) Island Skirmish in 1863. Sometimes the raiders got away with boat loads of food and even their former slaves. Whatever they did, the Union officers reported them as "very annoying" on more than one occasion.

General Thomas W. Sherman, making his first report on the successful completion of the expedition, said, "The effect of this victory is startling. Every white inhabitant has left the island . . . with all their immense property left to the pillage of hordes of disaffected blacks . . ."

He should have added, and hordes of undisciplined soldiers. Later his reports did mention his shame at the plundering by Union men and strictly forbade it, but to most of the victors all seemed fair prey. Hilton Head was now the supply base for blockading the whole southern coast, and Sherman set about organization. The name of Fort Walker he changed to honor Gideon Welles, U. S. Secretary of the Navy, and Fort Beauregard became Fort Seward. A few days later, Nov. 22, 1861, he ordered that the post office and townsite on Hilton Head near the fort be named Port Royal. From then on all official reports referred to Port Royal, rather than Hilton Head, and many people thought they were two different places, especially since Port Royal was already the name of the island on which Beaufort was located. The names of Welles and Seward soon slipped from common usage, but Port Royal remained the official designation for the town on Hilton Head—and for the whole area—till January, 1872, when Hilton Head was restored as title.

Now that the fortifications were well established, the main problem on the island was what to do with the Negroes. They were slaves without masters, in a slave state, held by conquerors who professed not to believe in slavery. Therefore they were not truly slaves, and yet they were not freed. "Contrabands of war," someone called them, and Contrabands they became in official parlance. Among them were some who were loyal to the families to which they had belonged, others were bitter and all were bewildered. Loyal or bitter, they could only wonder whether their old masters would return.

General Drayton, for instance. Right over there he had got down off that white horse and said, "I'll be back!" If he didn't come back, he was dead, sure. They talked it over. Somehow the picture grew of General Drayton entering the Kingdom of Heaven on a milk-white horse. The Lord would meet him, ready to anoint him with the sacred oil of the Scriptures. The words fit themselves to plaintive high-pitched music, and a new spiritual took form:

> Meet, O Lord, on de milk-white horse:
> An' de 'n'intin' wile* in de han'.
> Drop on, drop on de crown on my head.
> An' rolly* in my Jedus arms.
> In dat mornin' all day,
> In dat mornin' all day.
> In dat mornin' all day,
> When Jedus de Chris' been born.

A second verse followed, perhaps implying how long the boy had waited holding Drayton's horse after the battle was done:

> Moon went into de poplar tree
> An' star went into de blood . . .

The words and the story behind it were explained to the curious Northerners, and William Francis Allen wrote them down for his collection of slave songs heard at Port Royal. The last line with its "when Jedus de Chris' been born" suggests that the song may have been sung for the first time on Christmas Day. New York newspapers carried an account of the 1861 Christmas celebration and mentioned the singing by slaves on the Drayton plantation. The festival began with the tolling of a bell at eleven o'clock Christmas Eve, and at midnight a great fire was kindled in front of the "praise house"—the cabin used for religious services. The hymns were lined out by one of the three

Rolly means hold him; *'n'intin' wile* is anointing vial.

leaders and sung with fervor till about two in the morning when everyone stopped for coffee. Then came the "shout," and any of the soldiers who had been curious enough to stay awake and watch saw the black figures forming a circle, moving round and round the narrow space with a hitching, jerking motion, singing all the while, and those who did not join the shouters beat time with willing hands.

The new year brought many changes to this new island foothold in enemy territory. Carpenter shops and foundries were hastily constructed to service the blockading fleet. Officers' quarters were in the plantation Big Houses, but a great many other buildings were needed—hospitals, supply depots, barracks, a prison. Supply ships from the North arrived every day, discharged their cargo and returned to homeport, often laden with the bales of cotton appropriated from the vanquished. In May the port was declared open to foreign trade by Presidential proclamation and a customs house was erected.

Meanwhile Negroes had been flocking to the sea islands, certain that once they set foot on Yankee-held soil they would be free. The U. S. Treasury Department, eager to assure Negro labor to harvest the cotton of '61 and plant the new crop, assumed supervision. Secretary of the Treasury Chase was empowered on Nov. 30 to appoint a cotton agent and named Lt.-Col. W. H. Reynolds. On Dec. 3 General Thomas Sherman gave the same office to William H. Nobles, with James Adrian Suydam as assistant. The conflict was settled when Reynolds upheld Nobles' contract, granting him the additional right to confiscate and sell other products and property, as well as cotton, all on a five per cent commission. With this ample fee as incentive, Nobles was soon shipping pianos, furniture, private libraries and farm equipment along with the cotton. Shortly thereafter another conflict in authority came when Chase sent down Edward L. Pierce to supervise education of the contrabands and employ them in planting cotton. Pierce was far more interested in education than in cotton.

Since he had not been granted any money to pay teachers, Pierce appealed to benevolent societies in his home state of Massachusetts. In response an Educational Commission for Freedmen (later changed to the New England Freedmen's Aid Society) was promptly organized in Boston, and similar groups formed in Philadelphia and New York. They offered to pay prospective teachers a salary of $25 to $50 a month, while the Army guaranteed transportation and maintenance. Sixty-four men and women were in the first official group: 29 men and 4 women from Boston; 23 men and 8 women from New York and Washington. Many of the men were clergymen and others recent Harvard or Yale graduates. They sailed from New York in the steamer *Atlantic* on March 3, 1862, full of high ideals but not too much understanding of the task ahead. They called their project the "Port Royal Experiment" and their avowed purpose was to prove that cotton could be raised profitably by paid Negro labor, without driver's lash or force. Among them were some who burned with the added fervor of the Abolitionist. Aiding in the recruiting of this unusual band was Edward Everett Hale, the famous author, whose story "The Man Without A Country" had just been accepted by the *Atlantic Monthly*. One of Hale's special proteges was the Reverend Thomas Dwight Howard, who missed sailing with the first group when he was delayed by a Maine snowstorm.

When Tom Howard finally sailed on the steamer *Oriental*, some fifteen additional teachers were with him. After a few days in Beaufort they were assigned to various plantations and Howard found that his post was the farthest from Beaufort headquarters, on Hilton Head itself. Apparently one Negro school had already been opened on the island in January by a Mr. Barnard K. Lee, who came in advance of the sponsored group. But there were plenty of Negroes to be taught, and the young New England preacher found that teamed with him was a Mr. Strong, a former New York policeman who would superintend the farming. For quarters they were assigned to "the Widow Stoney's house," as Howard titled it in his memoirs, which would be Fairfield Plantation on Skull Creek some five miles west of the steamer landing. Of the five plantations assigned to his care Howard names only four: Stoney's, Pope's, Graham's and Stuart's. Since he adds that they were all contiguous, with Pope's the largest, the fifth was probably Muddy Creek Place or Jenkins Island. He adds that another large plantation was supervised by a Mr. Sanford, and that with him as teachers were Sanford's sister-in-law and another woman. By 1866 the New England Freedmen's Aid Society was sponsoring six teachers on Hilton Head, as well as others on St. Helena and elsewhere.

At the Widow Stoney's the New Englander found two officers of a Pennsylvania regiment already established, but there was room for all in the roomy, high-ceilinged house. Howard's diary does not describe the house fully, but we can picture it from letters of another teacher:

"The plantation houses are all built of hard pine, which is handsome on the floors, but the rest of the woodwork is painted . . . The walls are always left white . . . clapboards are unknown, but hard-pineboards a foot or more wide are put on in the same manner and everything outside is whitewashed. The place is very attractive-looking, with grapevines and honeysuckle, and pinewoods near. The house is raised high from the ground, as all are here, and boarded loosely underneath . . . The rooms are twelve feet high and the lower storey more than twelve feet from the ground. Some rooms are eighteen feet square . . . There's a circle of orange trees 'round the house and roses in abundance, but no grass. The quarters are a fourth of a mile or so from the house and a praise house stands near them."

Howard did mention admiringly that Rose of Sharon bushes grew almost as high as trees about the extensive grounds at Fairfield, and he described the lilting carol of the mockingbird and reported how much he enjoyed the delicious wild blackberries that grew everywhere in abundance. He must have felt a little homesick that first night, for he wrote wistfully that he could not see another house from his window. However, he was up early the next morning, ready for work. While Strong called in the farm hands and assigned tasks for the planting, the energetic Howard set out to count his pupils and parishioners. He preached his first service that Sunday in the praise house at Graham's, where the slaves had been accustomed to worship, but he held his first school in the best front parlor at Cotton Hope. The tabby foundations of that home still stand, half hidden by weeds and shrubbery, and they mark for present day visitors the site of one of the first Negro schools as well as one of the finest plantation homes. Other schools at Graham's and Stoney's were soon established, and the busy minister was pleasantly happy with his success at teaching his strange pupils to read and write.

In June the affairs of the refugees and abandoned lands was transferred from the Treasury to the War Department, and Mr. Howard was made administrative officer for the whole island, with headquarters at Fort Walker. Here he exchanged his lonely view of trees and flowers for the "stir and bustle of guard mounting and dress parades, together with the sound of axe and hammer in the building operations that were constantly going on." He also gave up his room at Fairfield for a home made of two tents, one of which served as office, the other as bedroom. At mealtime he joined a civilian mess headed by Mr. Severance, Collector of the Port, and served by a genial Negro "Aunty" famous for her gingerbread. Also in the group were a Mr. Wilson, superintendent of construction, Alfred Purdy, a clerk in the Custom House, several traders, a telegraph operator and four newspaper correspondents who daily grew more bored waiting for something decisive to happen in the unsuccessful siege of Charleston. Supervising Negro affairs now was Brigadier-general Rufus Saxton, formerly quartermaster for the Port Royal Expedition. His appointment relieved Pierce of further responsibility and his rank topped Reynolds, so both men soon left.

Military administration of the Department of the South also received a new chief. Thomas Sherman was transferred and to replace him came General David Hunter, a dark-eyed man of strong Abolitionist leanings. On May 9,

1862 he crystallized his sentiments with an unauthorized emancipation proclamation, much as Fremont had done in Missouri the previous August. Lincoln had ordered Fremont to withdraw his proclamation, and the President promptly published an annulment of Hunter's decree, also. In September Hunter was transferred on a temporary leave of absence to West Virginia, but before the transfer orders came through he drafted men for the first Negro troops in the United States Army and requisitioned red pantaloons to give them a distinguishing uniform. He did not manage to obtain formal orders to pay them, however, and there was much discussion throughout the nation as to whether Negroes should be allowed to fight, although they were eagerly accepted as laborers. One of the officers at Hilton Head, Charles Graham Halpine, wrote a humorous Irish dialect verse, "Sambo's Right to be Kilt," which was widely copied in Northern newspapers. Later, as public opinion changed, Negro troops were authorized, and Hilton Head claimed its early regiment as another "first." The officers of the regiment were all white men, with Colonel Thomas Wentworth Higginson in command, and Higginson's reports of Negro character were avidly read in the *Atlantic Monthly*.

Hunter's successor was General Ormsby Mitchell, for whom the island's Fort Mitchell was named. The ill-fated general died of yellow fever within six weeks, and the town around the fort was called Mitchellville in his memory, a name that would persist in local use long after the soldiers departed. After Mitchell's death General Brannan took over temporarily, but Hunter was eventually returned.

Hunter and Admiral Samuel F. Du Pont were supposed to be cooperating in using Hilton Head as a base for the capture of Charleston and Savannah. A signal tower was built on top of the Pope house at Coggins Point Plantation so that the two commanders could exchange messages with the new wigwag flags, but little cooperation was achieved and the Confederate ports were not taken. The general and the admiral wrote vindictive letters to Washington, each blaming the other. Both were relieved of their commands. The new chief of staff on Hilton Head was then General Quincy A. Gillmore, who had already served well in the department and had engineered a fort along Skull Creek named in his honor. For the Navy, Admiral Dahlgren took over.

Under Gillmore were more than 23,000 troops and when the sutlers and civilians were added to that number, there were more people on Hilton Head than would be seen here again for no one yet knows how many years. The civilian population increased as if by magic. Enterprising Yankee tradesmen swarmed in, wangled permission to open hotels, bars, photograph parlors, bakeries, drug stores, jewelry shops, bookshops, dry goods emporiums and shoe stores. The street on which the stores stood was named Sutlers' Row—soon changed to "Robbers' Row" in army slang. There was a post office, of course, and an American Express office, each in separate buildings. The first postmaster was Joseph Sears appointed Nov. 22, 1861, followed two years later by Barnard K. Lee, the teacher, and then by S. L. Brayton and Charles R. Brayton. Sears was also editor of the first newspaper on the island, the *New South*, published every Saturday morning, with offices on Union Square. Later a second paper, the *Palmetto Herald*, was started by the New York troops, with S. W. Mason and Co. as publishers, appearing every Thursday.

A few copies of these papers have been preserved in the Beaufort library and in the Georgia Historical Society at Savannah. (Colonial Dames Collection of Joshua Blackwood Howell Papers). From them we can catch a glimpse of the social life on Hilton Head in these war years, evidently quite gay in spite of the death and suffering that came with the bloody siege of Charleston.

The first wedding of the occupation days was that of T. J. Nungesser of the First New York Engineers and Miss Mary E. Shekell, formerly of St. Augustine, Florida, held on March 7, 1864. The ceremony was performed at the home of the bride's father, "located in the lumber yard." We can imagine the courting that went on before that day, aided—perhaps—by many a drink of the refresh-

ing soda water sold in stoneware bottles at Dr. Walsh's
drugstore. Plenty of that sparkling beverage—"in all the
best flavors"—must surely have been sold by the thriving
Dr. Walsh, for stoneware bottles are still washed in by
the tides or uncovered by the shifting sands near the old
fort. Here too have been found a druggist's mortar and
pestle and many a medicine bottle, some of which may have
come from the hospital instead of the druggist's shop.

A little more expensive courting could be done at one of
the island's three hotels—Port Royal House, Palmetto
House, and Sea Island Hotel—all of which advertised
themselves as rivaling the hostleries at Newport. An elaborate meal could also be obtained at the National Dining
Saloon, and all of these busy places advertised that their
fine meats and cheese were imported from New York, which
was only seventy hours away by regular steamer service,
and that their menus included the finest of imported wines.
Wine bottles of many shapes dug up on island shores nearly
a hundred years later well support that boast.

As further proof that these hotels did not lack for pa-
tronage is the item in the *Palmetto Herald* for April 30,
1864, informing us that Messrs. Gilson and Riddell, proprietors of the Port Royal House, were forced to add
another storey to accommodate guests. These guests, along
with any soldiers off duty, often found pleasant entertainment at the Union Theater, where an all-soldier cast put
on thrillers such as "The Spectre Bridegroom" and "The
Two Murders." Frequently registered on the hotel guest
books were Northern magazine and newspaper correspondents, for there was great interest in the "Port Royal Experiment" as well as in military maneuvers. The New York
Nation ran a weekly column called "The Freedmen" and
Harper's Monthly sent young Charles Nordhoff to report
the scene for its many readers.

Nordhoff took one of the regular steamers down to
Beaufort, but he had to do some fast talking to get a pass
to Fort Walker. The next boat leaving for the island was
the *Fah-kee*, carrying 300 barrels of gunpowder and 3,000
shells for the fort arsenal and no one wanted a civilian

aboard. Nordhoff managed to get permission, finally, but he had more fast talking to do when the provost marshal boarded the vessel at Seabrook Wharf. Once he was past that stern official he began filling his notebook:

"On every hand you see marks of long settlement. Live oaks, cedars, pines in long avenues leading up to the plantation houses and bounding the roads . . . Palmettoes—valuable as piles because the marine worm doesn't eat it, and for shade on fields because it doesn't grow fast or cast as much shade as live oaks . . . Yellow jessamine in bloom, smells like violets . . . roses . . . orange blossoms . . .

To a Northerner such flowers in March were unbelievable and the green-growing lushness of the whole island set him searching for adjectives that would make his readers see its beauty. Since this was wartime he also took note of the military aspects and mentioned that General Hunter and his wife held daily pistol practice on the beach in the early mornings, and that the lady was an excellent shot.

The thorough-going writer also took time to get acquainted with the enlisted men, one of whom asked him to mail a letter addressed thus:

To my own dear Biddy who is at home crying her eyes out because her own dear husband is in the Army.

Mr. Postmaster—Will you please be kind enough to hand this over to her immediately after it gets to Uniontown, Lafayette Co. Pennsylvania Ameriky.

So there were homesick boys in blue on Hilton Head as well as plundering vandals and abolitionists. Perfectly ordinary homesick boys, blue-eyed, brown-eyed, neither especially good nor bad, who remembered a wife's farewell kiss or mother's home cooking and who felt a lump in the throat as they sang "When this cruel war is over . . . "

The cruelty of the war had an aspect here on the sea islands that reached beyond the death and bloodshed of the battlefields. The land itself was forfeit. On June 7, 1862, Congress passed the necessary legislation whereby all occupied land was placed under a direct tax. If the tax was not paid, all lands and property thereon were forfeit to the United States government. Only two landholders in all Beaufort County paid this assessment. One was a Northerner named Eustis owning part of a plantation on Ladies Island. The only Southerner to pay was a Mr. Pritchard who lived on one of the Hunting Islands near Bay Point and had not escaped before Federal occupation. While Pritchard chose to take the required oath of allegiance to the Union and pay the tax rather than wage a one-man war, other landholders felt—quite reasonably— that they could not pay tax to an enemy government and still be loyal to the Confederacy. Furthermore, many of them probably did not even hear of the tax. True, a proper notice had been published in the Beaufort paper, but this was scarce likely to be read by soldiers in the Confederate Army or by women who had taken refuge in the interior. So, as the Northerners confidently expected, the tax went unpaid.

Since the Northerners were well aware that no Confederate could cross enemy lines to pay the tax without being captured, the assessment, for all its apparent legality, was equal to high-handed confiscation. If the land had merely been used to supply food and housing to the occupying forces, the action would have been simple war tactics. Armies were expected to live off the country they conquered. Also, President Lincoln himself had stipulated that forfeiture of any confiscated land was not meant to last longer than the secessionist owner's normal lifetime. Therefore, what happened next was unjust, unprecedented, unbelievable. The land was sold. Sold outright to Northern speculators and exploiters, to Negroes, the New England missionaries, teachers and cotton superintendents. With the land went the houses and barns, the family heirloom furiture abandoned in hurried flight, well-loved books in costly leather bindings, pianos, rugs, chandeliers, china. All were sold now with the plantations—unless, of course, they had already been stolen by Negroes or appropriated by the plunderers under Cotton Agent Nobles, who had made a

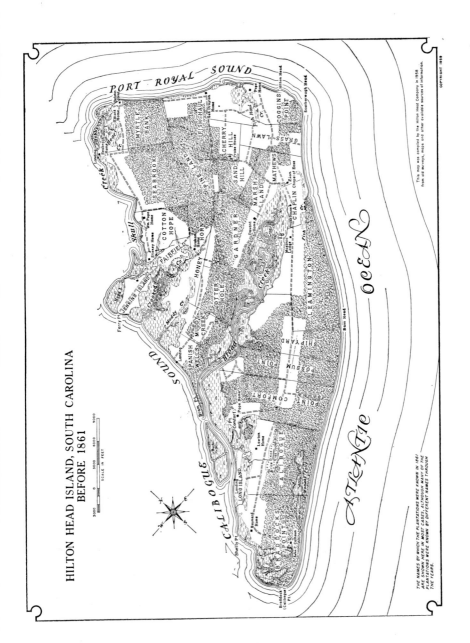

HILTON HEAD ISLAND, SOUTH CAROLINA
BEFORE 1861

This map was compiled by the Hilton Head Company in 1959
from old surveys, maps and other available sources of information.

THE NAMES BY WHICH THE PLANTATIONS WERE KNOWN IN 1861
ARE SHOWN WHERE KNOWN. OF COURSE, MANY OF THE
PLANTATIONS WERE KNOWN BY DIFFERENT NAMES THROUGH
THE YEARS.

COPYRIGHT 1959

MAP OF HILTON HEAD, SHOWING ITS TOPOGRAPHY.

Ladies News Magazine, 1861

Old Bottles Found at Site of Fort Walker — *Orion D. Hack*

good thing of that five per cent commission on the shipments he sent to New York.

A good many abolitionists felt that the land should not be sold, but given to the former slaves, and they urged the Negroes to stake out their claims. Speculators pulled political strings to regulate the selling price, and as a result the official orders to sell were sent out, recalled, sent out again with different wording, suspended for a time, reopened. Johnny-on-the-spot speculators and resident teachers and supervisors grabbed at the opportunity to buy this fabulous sea-island paradise for a dollar an acre, or perhaps a dollar and a quarter, house, barns, tools and livestock thrown in. Some of the Negroes who had been hoarding the money earned as laborers or from selling high-priced fish, vegetables and poultry to the Yankees now stepped forward and plunked down hard cash. Something over forty plantations went to white men and only six to the freed blacks.

On Hilton Head the sales were declared open December first, 1863. On December 2, Freeman Dodd bought the one thousand acres of Graham's Honey Horn for $200. On the following February 20 Dodd sold it to Ramon Rivas for $10,000. Who Dodd was or what he did with his booty is not recorded. But it is known that Rivas sold half the land quickly for its purchase price and that he held on to the remaining 500 acres for over a year, selling it for a profit of $4,725 above its cost. The couple who paid him this fancy price, Ana and Robustrand Hergues, then paid nearly twice as much for the other half of Honey Horn. No doubt they expected to make a profit of their own with crops of sea-island cotton, but such was not the case. Cotton which sold at a dollar a pound in 1865 dropped to sixty-six cents the next year and brought a beggarly four cents by 1890. Meanwhile, there were poor crops on Hilton Head, for the fields were plagued with weevils and damp, as well as Yankees. Furthermore, most of the best seed was lost when the crops of 1861 were sent North to be ginned, and as Elliott had long ago pointed out, careful selection of seed was the all-important secret of success. By 1870 the Hergueses would give up and sell the land to Edward and Eugenia Valentine for only $7,800. A coffin marked "Remains of M. Hergues" found in the Baynard vault in Zion churchyard indicates that they may have lost a child, as well as a fortune.

Meanwhile other plantations on Hilton Head fell under the auctioneer's mallet or were acquired less openly. A group of investors styling themselves "The Sea Island Company" bought Gardner's, Muddy Creek Place, Otter Hole and Leamington. In an old record book found in a building at Otter Hole we can read their inventory for 1866:

> *Gardner's*
> 550 acres arable land (cotton) ....$ 100 per acre
> 874 acres timber land ....   55 per acre
> 1 mansion $4,000
> 25 freedmen's houses.............$7,500
> 1 cotton drying arbour ....$ 500
> 1 horse barn, very large $3,000

Also listed: hog pen, beehives, plows, seed, clothing, tools, tobacco, brooms, blacksmith shop, carpenter shop, etc. for a total of nearly 300 items.

At Stuart's no mansion was mentioned, possibly because it had been burned in wartime, but there were 14 freedmen's houses, 400 acres of cotton land and 500 acres of timber. At Muddy Creek Place was a dwelling place, rather than a mansion, 14 freedmen's houses, 450 acres of cotton land and 294 of timber. Leamington comprised 450 acres of arable land and 984 acres of timber, and all of the land was given about the same valuation as that recorded for Gardner's, no small total.

Evidence of the falling price of cotton comes in the inventory for these same lands only twelve years later, when the new owners are described as "The United States Cotton Company." Land had dropped sharply in value from $100 an acre to $15 or $20 for cotton land and $5 for timber acres. The Gardner mansion was appraised at only one-fourth its former value. The difference may be partially accounted for if this second inventory is an operating appraisal while the former was a touched-up seller's price list, but even with this allowance it is evident that something had changed the get-rich quick optimism on Hilton Head, something more than falling cotton prices.

The change was no doubt due in part to the Special Field Order No. 15 issued January 16, 1865, by General William Tecumseh Sherman, in charge of the final devastation in the South. This order limited the sale of all sea-island land to Negroes only. In addition it also set aside a strip of mainland thirty miles in width along the coast from Charleston to the St. John's River in Florida, comprising the best of the rice-growing lands, for Negro purchasers only. Loyal white Northerners who had already bought property in this restricted area were allowed to continue ownership, but no new sales to white persons could be made. The order was made partly to take care of the thousands of Negro refugees who had attached themselves to Sherman's marching army and had to be provided for, fed, clothed, given work and a home. It was also an attempt to insure that the land would be sold in the small ten-and twenty-acre plots that Negroes could afford instead of in the 500-acres-and-up lots coveted by speculators. Conceivably, there was also the idea that this chopping up of the large plantations would make it more difficult for the Confederates to reclaim their holdings when the war was over, and surely Sherman knew that the end of the war was in sight.

Previous legislation had already limited land sales to twenty acres for each adult male, plus twenty more if he were married, but the order had not been followed too literally. A further restriction required each purchaser to have lived in the occupied territory six months prior to purchase. Soldiers, sailors and marines were allowed double the quantity granted to civilians and there were evidently no restrictions placed on re-sale to speculators. Sherman's order put a stop to these sales, and the new purchases made by Negroes soon came under the auspices of the newly organized Freedmen's Bureau, headed by General O. O. Howard. Howard had been appointed by President John-

son, who understood he was Lincoln's choice, and the new
chief had orders to sell the confiscated lands in lots of not
more than forty acres to a family or to rent it to them with
a three-year option to buy later. On Hilton Head, Howard's agent was the same General Rufus Saxton appointed
by General Hunter to handle Negro affairs in the early
days of occupation. His territory extended to all of South
Carolina, Georgia and Florida and he soon reported that
he had disposed of 485,000 acres of land to 40,000 Negroes. The three tax commissioners indicated the land to
be sold and the government surveyors marked out the
boundaries in hurried haphazardry and the diagram of land
sales on Hilton Head soon resembled a patchwork crazy
quilt.

The decline in island real estate values may also be
blamed on the end of the war and the inevitable suspicion
that the former owners might be reinstated after all. Letters home to New England frequently mentioned this pos-
sibility and the new owners were by no means as certain of
their rights of tenure as they pretended to be. Lee sur-
rendered only three months after Sherman's Negroes-only
order was issued and final capitulation would take a scant
two months more. President Johnson proclaimed his policy
of amnesty to the secessionists and their right to regain
their property on pledging allegiance to the Union. However the Port Royal area was still a Yankee stronghold,
with Union troops in residence, and this fact gave the new
landholders confidence.

In May the Confederate President Jefferson Davis was
captured and rumor spread that he would be brought to the
prison at Hilton Head, where many Southern sympathizers
had been housed throughout the war. On May 15, 1865,
an exctied group of civilians and soldiers gathered at the
wharf near Fort Walker to watch the riverboat carrying
Davis and other prisoners come alongside. The watchers got
only a glimpse of the important captives, however, for the
party was quietly transferred to the steamer *Clyde* bound
for Fortress Monroe in Virginia: Jefferson Davis, his wife
Varina Howell Davis and their children, Vice President
Alexander Stephens, Senator and Mrs. Clay, Colonel Bur-

ton Harrison, Colonel Lubbock, Postmaster-general Reagan, Colonel W. P. Johnson, General Joseph Wheeler. Only a few Negroes came ashore. These were the former servants of Mrs. Davis, who sent a note asking Saxton to grant them whatever benefits were now due to former slaves. Then the prison ship sailed on, guarded by the gunboat *Tuscarora,* and Hilton Head began to realize that it would have to adjust to peace time.

Would the Confederate landowners return and could they regain their property if they did come? That was the question of the hour. Saxton claimed that Sherman's Order took precedence over the President's proclamation of amnesty and that all the new wartime land titles on the sea islands were legal, unchangeable. The President had Saxton removed, and his successor, Robert K. Scott, then ruled that dispossessed owners might return, but that no Negroes could be evicted. Apparently that satisfied Johnson but it did not give the old landowners much reason for coming back. Many who returned found their old homes burned, half torn down or occupied by Negroes or Northerners. Widows and children, deprived of inheritance, took what charity was offered by friends and kinsmen. Most of the men who returned took bitter survey and moved elsewhere.

Other confiscated land throughout the south was restored with more or less reasonable promptness, but by 1872 much of the sea-island acreage was still held by wartime title and by the Federal government itself. Special legislation was finally passed by Congress to correct this injustice, and the abandoned lands could be re-possessed by paying the old wartime tax, plus interest. However, even this face-saving legal remedy was of no avail to persons whose lands had already been sold. Those unfortunate families had to be content with a meager reimbursement of $5 per acre for cultivated fields, $1 for timberland. Even families whose lands remained unsold sometimes had difficulty claiming them. Often they did not have the ready cash after all the war years of sacrifice and hardship. Often there was delay in proving ownership, especially when the pre-war owner was dead and his will, written to distribute considerable wealth, now had to be applied to poverty. Furthermore, clear titles could not be obtained in Beaufort County, for all the records had been destroyed when Gillisonville, the old county seat, came in the path of Sherman's march. Luckily, some of the families had wills or proof of title recorded in other counties. The Elliotts, Lawtons and Matthews were able to regain almost all their former holdings. The Draytons, Popes and Baynards obtained only part, while the Gardners actually got none of their former plantation but did manage to buy land nearby. No other pre-war families seem to be listed in the purchasers of Redemption Certificates of the 1870's. Perhaps others were discouraged when any chance to prove that land was still unsold vanished when the county records of Federal land sales and surveys burned to ashes in Beaufort, the new county headquarters. Had the blaze been set on purpose to cover illegal transactions and prevent further claims? Many Southerners believed so. Officially there was no investigation. Right or wrong, the contemporary occupants on Hilton Head were adjudged rightful landowners. The Redemption Act had at least taken the first step on the road back to prosperity. There was a long way to go.

CHAPTER VIII

THE
AFTERMATH

IN THE poverty-ridden postwar year of 1867 the Reverend James Stoney returned to St. Luke's Parish and preached once again in the Church of the Cross at Bluffton. He also tried to hold services in Zion Chapel of Ease on Hilton Head, but there were not enough worshippers to support a church. Evidently there were few Episcopalians anywhere in the parish, for the church of St. Luke's on Euhaw Road was sold to the Methodists in 1875, and Methodist it still remains. However, the graveyard north of the chapel was reserved for former communicants of St. Luke's, and there they still lie beneath moss-covered headstones. Zion Chapel on Hilton Head stood empty, unused.

When the Reverend James Stoney entered the chapel on his last visit to the island he may have felt a premonition that its doors would never again open to holy service. The lovely silver chalices of the Communion Service, brought from England in 1834 had already disappeared. No doubt they were stolen soon after the fall of Fort Walker. When next heard of they would be in a pawnshop covered with dust and tarnish, and the man who bought them there mistook them for antique goblets. When the tarnish was removed he was amazed to see the sacred Christian symbols and the words "Zion Capel of Ease . . .

Hilton Head." There was only one thing for a Christian
to do—return them to their rightful altar. But by this
time neither the altar nor the chapel remained on Hilton
Head. Soon after Stoney's last visit in 1867 the abandoned
building had been torn down by pilfering hands and the
doors, windows, benches, the very boards and roof shingles
were taken away, no doubt to serve in some freedman's
cabin. Even the foundation stones disappeared. The
ground was plowed over for planting and soon nothing
was left to mark the site. Only the gravestones in the churchyard stood unmolested in lonely silence beneath the moss-
hung branches. In time the coffins of the Baynard mausoleum disappeared. The iron railing around the Kirk
family plot rusted, crumbled. There was no longer a place
on Hilton Head for silver Communion chalices. Would
there ever be? Hopefully, the purchaser of the chalices put
them in the custody of St. Helena's Church in Beaufort,
where so many island families had worshipped through the
early years. There they still remain, but some day they
may yet be reconsecrated before a new altar on Hilton
Head. It is where they belong.

Some of the family silver from Hilton Head homes
found its way to pawnshops, also. Some of it was taken
there by the vandals who stole it, but perhaps even more
was bartered by hungry owners. Women and children—
even men—have to eat. With lands confiscated and savings
given to the war effort, only family treasures remained to
exchange for bread. More than one family legend tells of
sparkling jewels or shining silver snatched at the last moment of flight from Hilton Head. Grandmother Elliott
was one who had the presence of mind to have the silver
ready to go, packed carefully in an old cowhide trunk.
Some of it had been in the family for generations, brought
from England with the earliest of the colonists. Let the
booming Yankee guns threaten ever nearer. She would
not go without her treasured silver. And she did not. The
cowhide trunk rode with her in the boat that carried her
to the mainland, never out of her sight one moment. In
the kinsman's house where she found refuge, the trunk was

1898 Dynamite Gun Emplacement

Kenneth Rogers

Drayton's "Fish Haul" in the 1860's

S. C. Historical Society

Group Being Addressed by Will Clyde, about 1900

carefully hidden, and Grandmother never let anyone doubt that one day the silver would again grace an Elliott table with its shining loveliness. Long years after the war was over Elliott heirs would be hunting that cowhide trunk, certain that it still contained family treasure. Others shook their heads. No use to look. Even if the gallant old lady had never admitted it, the silver must have been sold to eke out the poverty of reconstruction. There could have been no other way.

Poverty demanded much that would never have been believed in other days. A son of the Elliott's was actually making fishing his livelihood, not a pastime. He sold his catch, furthermore, to the officers' mess at Fort Walker, carrying it there himself with a face schooled to blankness. General Gillmore discovered his identity and promptly insisted that the former enemy be treated as an officer and gentleman. Gillmore also secured Elliott's official pardon, restoring citizenship. Shortly thereafter Gillmore was transferred to another post.

Even the restoration of property did not alleviate such need, for the families who regained their lands under the Redemption Act of 1872 found that they were not free to manage their estates. Wages to freedmen, working contracts and rents all were under the control of the Freedmen's Bureau. While the principle behind these restrictions may have been just, practical application was not, and the planters often had difficulty in making even the barest living. Something of their struggle can be glimpsed in the pages of the *Charleston News and Courier* for March 23, 1878, as we read the speech delivered by the Reverend Charles Pinckney, son of Caroline Elliott of Hilton Head and C. C. Pinckney of Pinckney Island. We can almost hear the bitter overtones that must have been in the man's low-pitched resonant voice as he spoke of the ruined ghost houses he had seen on his return to Hilton Head in 1874. Almost nothing was left there to remind him of the happy times when he had visited Grandmother Elliott at Myrtle Bank. The house itself had burned down. Its lonely chimneys stood "like sorrowing sentinels over the desolate ground." Even the famous myrtle along the banks had vanished, and the banks themselves had been washed away in the violent sea storms that had added to man-made destruction. Fire from the burning house had spread to the garden, scorching some of the shade trees. The sea had swallowed others, even the massive live oaks. But along the garden walk the yellow jonquils and bright-hued iris had sprung up to bloom as gaily as always. They were the only touch of welcome he found on that sorry day of homecoming.

He turned from the ruins of Myrtle Bank to visit the other plantations he had known so well and to seek shelter for the night. Not one house was occupied by its rightful owner. Some, like Myrtle Bank, were only charred ruins. Some were occupied by Negroes and others stood stripped and tenantless. Only one door opened to a familiar face.

Although the minister, with the reticent gentility of his era, mentioned no name, the familiar face was surely that of Eugenia Valentine, then mistress of Honey Horn. The Reverend Mr. Pinckney said only that the home was one bought by a New Yorker for his southern bride, and his audience needed no further identification. Their talk that night, Pinckney added, turned to Robinson Crusoe, the prisoner of Chillon and other lonely persons, for his hostess revealed that in the past four years she had seen but one other white gentlewoman, she had not attended a single church service nor paid a social call. Perhaps there was more friendliness in the remaining years of the fourteen she spent there, but there was surely not much profit, for the home was lost to a foreclosed mortgage.

The deep-voiced minister went on to tell of his own experiences as a planter. Once his plantation had brought a yearly profit of $10,000. Now he was allowed to collect $300 in yearly rents from his Negro tenants, if all the houses were occupied. Many were not in these years, for the freedmen went eagerly to work in the new sea-island phosphate mines where wages were high and the task more adventuresome than familiar farming. In that year of 1878 Pinckney's agent had collected $122.25, and the next day in Beaufort he had paid his tax assessment of $120.05. The balance in hand was not likely to make shabby gentility less shabby. "What the upper millstone spares, the nether crushes," he said. Still, he counseled courage. With resolute hearts, with active hands, with friendly laws and the blessing of heaven the land would smile again.

His prophecy was not fulfilled. When the Valentines lost their home in 1884, the new owner was a land-hungry Northern speculator, the merchant F. R. Klem, whose name was on many another deed of sale. If the land was smiling again, it was on Northerners and Negroes only. The picture of Hilton Head in 1888 comes from the diary of the missionary-teacher Reverend Thomas Howard who came back in that year to show his wife the lovely, flower-filled island he had known and loved in wartime.

They came in March and the skies were not softly blue as he had boasted they would be. Dark and threatening clouds greeted them as they stepped down from the train at Beaufort. Some days later when word came that a wind-whipped blizzard howled over New York, they realized that Carolina was treating them very kindly after all. They took the early morning steamer for Hilton Head and stood by the rail eager for the sight of the long pier where the minister had first disembarked. The pier was not there. It had been washed away, someone explained, and never replaced. There was no need for it now. Nobody went to old Port Royal any more, or almost nobody. Not only was Fort Walker abandoned, but a good share of the parade grounds and part of the old general hospital had been washed away.

There was another steamer landing farther along Skull Creek, however, and the elderly couple stepped ashore near the Widow Stoney house where the teacher had first been billeted. A Negro drove them to Merchants' Row, where shop doors stood open beneath the shade of white-washed lattice arcades and rustling palmettoes. Howard inquired for any former pupils, and the merchant Klem sent for those he knew. Some had drifted away, but many remained on their freedmen's plots, still living from the land and the sea, still eager for their children to have book learning. Perhaps there were three thousand Negroes on the island, all told, the merchant estimated.

No doubt the kindly minister also visited the post office supervised by W. J. Fripp, for the postmaster was always the center for exchange of island news. "Hilton Head" was now the correct postal term, instead of the confusing wartime "Port Royal," although in local talk the old army name of Mitchellville was often used. Other postmasters who had served there since war days were the merchant John Franz, appointed July 15, 1867; Francis Wilder—who declined and retired to live on his plantation at Otter Hole—Robert C. McIntire, postwar owner of Seabrook's, Fairfield, Grasslawn and other acreage; then William R. Kennison and Gabriel P. Gardner.

In addition to F. R. Klem the New England visitors may have met another confirmed islander, W. D. Brown. The Browns had bought Cherry Hill, Possum Point and Mathew's Field, and they soon opened a general store that would eventually become the island post office, with Mrs. Lulie Brown in charge and her husband named as assistant. They had two pretty daughters—Fanny and Helen—and all of them loved the island's quiet green peace, its meadows, woodlands and white sand shores.

The island was truly quiet again after the soldiers went away. In time even the soldiers' graves would be moved to the National Cemetery at Beaufort. The birds and the small woodland animals were not long in reclaiming their old haunts. Great flocks of ducks came again to winter in the island marshes and feed on the sawgrass, duck weed and other swamp plants. Mallard drakes with glistening green heads lording it over their drab-feathered mates. Long-necked, graceful pintails. Redheads. Canvas-backs. Gadwalls. Shovellers with the wide bills. Widgeons, teal, wood duck, scaups, ringnecks, buffleheads, mergansers and the tip-tail ruddy ducks. The deer increased, also, and there were plenty of raccoons, wild hogs, squirrels and rat-tailed opossums among the thickets. Quail, marsh hens, doves and wild turkeys roamed the fields.

Hunters from the mainland came, of course. Many of them were older men who went home boasting that the game on Hilton Head was more plentiful than it had ever been, even in their boyhood. Several of them banded together as the "Beaufort Club" and bought 1000 acres of what had once been Leamington, buying the right to hunt where their fathers had once been welcome guests or generous host. After some years they sold their preserve to a group of hunters from North Carolina, who bought additional land to double the acreage.

Word of the huntsman's plenty on Hilton Head, the sunny skies and mild winters spread northward, and shortly before 1890 a New Englander named W. P. Clyde began acquiring land on Hilton Head, piece by piece, till he owned 9000 acres. He kept this island domain for hunting and for sun-lazy vacations, making the house at Honey Horn his headquarters, for that was the only one of the antebellum houses still standing and usable. With him was J. E. Lawrence as superintendent and the yellow-bearded Henry Padgett as game keeper. Another investor, J. L. Dimmock, also bought considerable acreage in 1896.

The most memorable event of these years was the hurricane of 1893. For years afterward, islanders dated births, deaths, marriages and other events as taking place so long before or after the "Big Blow". The Red Cross sent Clara Barton to direct relief, and Joel Chandler Harris wrote of the disaster for *Scribner's Magazine*.

Throughout all these years of peace the Federal government had still kept possession of the 803 acres at Coggins Point where Fort Walker was located. During the war days of 1898 when there was once again threat of Spanish invasion, the fort was reactivated and a new-type dynamite gun installed. The threat was short lived. The war ended and the buildings were turned over to the quartermaster's department, empty and abandoned, on August 17, 1899. The land remained government property and the Pope family had no chance of reclaiming it.

As Clyde grew older he began selling some of his many acres on Hilton Head, although keeping hunting rights for

as long as he wished to use them. Another Northerner, Roy
Rainey, began acquiring island property in large amounts.
The plantation of Otter Hole changed hands, going to
W. L. Hurley of New Jersey, although its former owner,
F. E. Wilder, reserved the right to occupy the house as
long as he lived. The Hurleys moved in on a grand scale,
with a yacht at anchor in Broad Creek and an automobile—
ferried cross with much excited interest—in the shed. They
soon added part of Muddy Creek Place and Gardner's to
their estate to total 1700 acres and the inventory mentioned
turkeys, chickens, horses, mules and wagons as well as the
house, yacht and auto.

The famous long-staple sea-island cotton was still growing on Hilton Head at the beginning of the twentieth century, and urged on by the demands of World War I, new
planters came to the island in the new war years. The Mac-
Donald-Wilkins Company of Savannah owned or leased
a good part of Fairfield and other nearby fields from 1913
to their bankruptcy in the depression year of 1932. The
partners in this concern were M. D. Batchelder, William
Keyserling and G. W. Wilkins.

When the United States joined the Allies in 1917, the
abandoned barracks at Coggins Point were cleaned and re-
paired and the big guns were fitted to their emplacements.
Troops came but did not stay long, although they kept
lookout for enemy submarine attack right up till Armistice
Day. Then the soldiers left again and once more the island settled back to its peaceful somnolence. The long-
staple cotton was gone now, also, the last of its precious
seed destroyed by the ruthless boll weevil, not only on Hilton Head but on all of the sea islands. It would not return.
There was no longer any glittering, get-rich-from-cotton
promise to lure planters to the Carolina-Georgia coast.

The hopeful phosphate mining boom had faded, too,
dimmed by the discovery of easier-to-mine ore in Florida,
and fishing became the chief island industry. Shrimp and
oysters were the catch most sought after, although plenty
of winter trout, sea bass, sheepshead and other fish were
available. For some time there were only two men on the

island who made sea-food packing a business. One was James B. Hudson, who owned part of Fairfield and would also serve as postmaster in later years. The other was S. V. Toomer who came to Hilton Head about 1912 and bought a tract he called Hickory Bluff, between the main road and Jarvis Creek, as well as other plots at various times.

In 1923 probably the best known white man on the island was W. D. Brown. "Old Man Brown" everyone called him. Both his daughters were married now and living on the mainland, but he and his wife still ran their general store and Lulie Brown was still postmistress, as she had been ever since 1907 when Sarah Heywood resigned. The Negroes came to Brown for help with their problems and often he acted as banker. Consequently on Saturday nights, or almost any night if he hadn't been to the mainland recently, Old Man Brown was likely to have a good bit of money in the till. He never worried about it, just carried it upstairs and put it in the box beneath his bed. It never occurred to him that the Negroes might try to rob him some dark night. Probably it never occurred to the Negroes, either. They had always been a law-abiding lot, sincere in their efforts to seek—and find—religion. Brown had helped two different congregations obtain land for their churches, selling them some of his own holdings at a reasonable price. In their island isolation, Hilton Head Negroes were almost like one family, everyone always knew what everyone else was doing and any rare stranger from the mainland was quickly spotted. Like those two colored men who came over on July third. Could be they were someone's kinfolk, arriving for the holiday.

There wasn't much holiday celebration, of course, on sleepy Hilton Head. The two Brown daughters, Helen Campbell and Fannie Holmes, decided to stay in Beaufort for the fireworks, where there were parties and visitors all over town. After midnight someone in Beaufort happened to glance toward Hilton Head. The sky over the island was lit by a red glare. Fireworks? They looked again, called others. That was not the sparkling blaze of Roman candles and set pieces, but the steady, burning glare of a

real fire. Those in Beaufort could only watch and wonder, but on Hilton Head people scrambled into their clothes,
leaped on horses or mules or ran down the dirt roads with
frightened, long-legged gait. No need to ask, "Where's
the fire?" It could be only one place—Old Man Brown's
store.

The store was a blazing bonfire before even the nearest
Negroes arrived. Bigger than all the Fourth of July and
New Year's Eve bonfires put together. Too late to drag
out the old man's favorite chair, the family clock, the . . .

Word died away on frightened lips, and black faces
turned to one another in terrified understanding. It was
even later than that. It was too late to save the Browns
themselves.

The fire died down, finally. Lawrence and Padgett—
the two white men who took care of Clyde's property—
were automatically in charge when the ashes were cool
enough to allow a search for the charred bodies. The
bodies were found. Both skulls were smashed by death-
dealing axe or club. No wonder the Browns had not awak-
ened. Murder. There were murderers on Hilton Head.

The two strangers. Everyone thought of them now.
No one had given them shelter. No one had helped them
leave. No one claimed kinsip or even acquaintance. Feverishly the distraught islanders thrashed through the under-
brush, searching for them, beating through the marsh grass,
stirring up rattlesnakes and indignant cotton mouths but
no murdering humans. Finally someone spotted the
dangling rope of a stolen rowboat and knew the criminals
had escaped. The search was turned over to the police on
the mainland and the murderers were soon tracked down.
One of them was boldly wearing a watch with the victim's
name engraved on the cover, and both confessed how they
had hidden in the nearby church loft while the fire burned,
how they had escaped in the stolen boat while searchers were
far afield. Execution followed conviction and the case
was closed.

Meanwhile, back on Hilton Head the island Negroes
kept well away from the ghostly ruins, although there

Will Clyde and Party

One-room Island School, 1955 — *S. C. Development Board*

Prehistoric Tooth Found on the Island

Melted Pennies found in ashes of Post Office fire, 1823.

Carl Woodring

were lengths of chain, a few hammers and axe heads and other bits of debris that could have been put to good use. A week after the Fourth when William Clyde and his friend J. G. Gemmell came down for a little hunting, the ruins were still untouched and Gemmell picked up a roll of pennies overlooked by the murderers, or dropped in guilty flight. In the heat the coins had fused together into an almost solid cylinder, with only narrow grooves to indicate the separate pieces. The penny on one end bore the date 1917, on the other was 1911. Gemmell put them into his pocket for a souvenir and nearly a quarter century later he would ask if there were a museum on Hilton Head to display them. Part of the Brown property went to the Osprey Club, Dr. T. E. Oertel, trustee. The club sold out to Roy Rainey in 1927. Rainey's holdings were extensive but short-termed, for by 1931 he sold out to two men who undertook to purchase almost the entire island — Landon K. Thorne and Alfred L. Loomis. These two Northerners even acquired the last piece of the confiscated property taken by the Federal government at the fall of Fort Walker in 1861. This last plot, the 803 acres of Coggins Point, had been declared a military reservation in 1874 and was finally offered for sale by the Secretary of War in 1927 at the price of $12,600. Thorne and Loomis also began buying land from any Negroes willing to sell, and by 1936 there were only 300 Negroes on the island instead of the 3,000 of forty years before.

Hunting was good on Hilton Head in these years. The gamekeeper flushed 293 covies of quail in the fall of 1936. As many as four thousand widgeons came to winter in the marshes and there were 18 or 20 other kinds of ducks, besides a flock of Canada geese. There were deer and wild turkeys aplenty. The big kitchen at Honey Horn sent out tempting fragrance of roast turkey and venison, of duck with orange sauce made from the bittersweet island oranges, Carolina shrimp pie, oysters stewed with crisp bacon and onions and served with fluffy rice. There was crunchy benne seed candy in the crystal dish, or perhaps a plate of pecan pralines, with the nuts fresh and crisp from island trees.

The new owners loved the island and tried to find out more of its history, more of the men and women who had once lived in the Big Houses that were now in ruins or completely obliterated. There was also a practical reason for delving into history. Eventually the land would be sold and purchasers would want a clear title, with names of previous owners and dates of sale. Because the land records of Beaufort County had twice been destroyed, a complete history was not possible, but as nearly as the truth was known—or indicated—it was recorded. An artist was commissioned to paint a map showing the ante-bellum plantations and the finished picture still hangs in the hall at Honey Horn. Another map of colonial times is displayed in the living room, with the title "Trench Island," and old diaries and magazine sketches that tell of historic days at Hilton Head are on the book shelves.

The post office at Hilton Head continued open for business, and serving it were William W. Wilcox from 1935 to 1938, William Barr from 1938 to 1941 and Leanella Greiner in 1941 and 1942. Succeeding her was Miss Beatrice Milley, who had come to the island as a young girl when her retired doctor-father rented the house at Otter Hole. She has kept a keen interest in island affairs and her collection of military relics found on Hilton Head dates from four wars.

The kinds of military insignia likely to be found on the island increased in World War II when U. S. Marines were stationed here. There were new gun emplacements on the ocean shore near Bass Head and the Leamington lighthouse, with barracks nearby. The base was often known as Camp Dilling, evidently because it was on former Dilling property, but according to the Department of Military History its title was Camp McDougal. This camp was used by the U. S. Coast Guard through 1943 when it was garrisoned by a Marine caretaking unit, then abandoned.

Meanwhile Thorne and Loomis families continued their delving into island history and what they had learned of the secession and postwar residents can be summed up here augmented by the research of many others:

PLANTATION SUMMARY

1. BAYNARD. *Spanish Wells* (600A). *Muddy Creek* (850A), *Braddock Point* (1000A).

Thomas Baynard of Edisto Island bought Spanish Wells Plantation before 1792, the year in which his brother William bought the adjoining Muddy Creek Place. Both were inherited by Thomas's son, William Eddings Baynard (1800-1849), who also owned Braddock's Point. Son William married Catherine Adelaide Scott, evidently an island girl herself. They had three daughters, Cecilia, Elizabeth, and Florence, who married the three Willingham brothers, and an elder daughter, Juliana, who married Wilson Hall and then Stephen Ellis. There were two sons, Ephraim and Joseph, both of whom married and had children. The Baynards also owned Buckingham Plantation with the mainland ferry landing, and other mainland property. They evidently purchased Spanish Wells from the Mongins, who may have had it from Roger Moor. Catherine survived her husband, dying in 1856, but William's will had already provided that the estate be divided among his sons and their children. In August 1875 Joseph S. Baynard, Sarah Baynard Guerard, Adelaide Baynard Guerard, Mary C. Baynard, Josephine Baynard Rogers, William E. Baynard, Ephraim M. Baynard, Elizabeth D. Baynard, Emma C. Baynard, Josephine A. Dickey and Amlin D. Baynard filed a petition to regain Spanish Wells and Braddock's Point under the Redemption Act, and did so by paying $533.41 in taxes. Muddy Creek Place, sold in wartime to the Sea Island Cotton Co., resold to the United States Cotton Co. and then to J. L. Dimmock who disposed of it in small plots, was not redeemable. In 1893 Elizabeth Baynard Ullmer filed suit against the other heirs to establish the claim of the children of the deceased Ephraim to share in the estate. The court ordered the land sold to satisfy her claim, and in 1894 both plantations were bought by W. P. Clyde.

2. CHAPLINS. *Chaplin's* (400A), *Marshlands* (400A). The Chaplins owned land on St. Helena Island and which of the brothers came to Hilton Head is not clear. Their

126   *Hilton Head*

plantation between Leamington and Mathews' contained 400 acres which was increased to 800 with the purchase of Marshlands, adjacent inland to their original purchase, and formerly owned by Thomas Webb, husband of Lydia Davant, and their son Samuel. Both estates were reserved by the Federal govenment for sale to Negroes and were not redeemable.

3. DRAYTON. *Fish Haul* (700A), *Pine Barrens* (400A) William Drayton and his wife Mary were owners of 1100 acres, 700 of which were the original Fish Haul Creek Plantation (often written "Fish Hall") probably bought from Samuel Green heirs about 1770, and the remaining 400 acres were the pine barrens or pineland tract to the northwest, bought shortly after 1856 from Daniel Jenkins and Harriett Pinckney. Part of this estate was sold by the Federal government to Negroes and part kept for a military reservation. The remainder was redeemed March, 1875 for $407.83 in taxes by the heirs of Mary (Drayton) Pope who had evidently remarried. The heirs were John E. Drayton, Anna Drayton Thomas, John Thomas, William S. Drayton, Mary Drayton, Percival Drayton, Emma Drayton, Thomas Fenwick Drayton, and they offered to give land for a new cemetery and for a church also if next-of-kin would remove bodies buried near their home. In 1877 the heirs began selling in small plots and in 1931 Thorne and Loomis bought Fish Haul land in thirteen different transactions.

4. ELLIOTT. *Myrtle Bank* (1000A). William Elliott of cottongrowing fame died in 1808 while being carried by boat from the island to Beaufort. His will stipulated that Myrtle Bank (half of which was the original Barnwell grant bought by his wife's family) be sold by his widow to son William. William, author of the devil-fishing exploits, did buy the land on Hilton Head and owned some of the other family land on the mainland as well. He and his wife Anne Hutchinson Smith Elliott had seven children, among them another William who inherited the purchase-right to Myrtle Bank. Wartime confiscation intervened and prevented purchase. Some plots were bought

by Negroes. Widow Anne attempted to regain the rest by tax redemption in 1874, but cash bequests in her husband's will forced the court to order the land sold. Daughters Anne and Emily bought Myrtle Bank at sheriff's sale in 1884 for $1000. Being unmarried, they bequeathed it to the children of their sister Harriott and the Cuban patriot general Ambrosio Jose Gonzales. Thorne and Loomis bought it from the Gonzales heirs in 1934.

5. FICKLINGS. (465A. or more) *Possum Point, Shipyard.* Both William and Samuel Fickling resided on Hilton Head in 1798. William's heirs are not traced. Samuel and wife Elizabeth Davant had three children — Jeremiah, William and Mary Anne. They may have sold their land at Possum Point and Shipyard before secession, as the map prepared for Sherman in November 1861 puts the name "Wills" at Possum Point. The Navy map of 1873 wrote "Wells." Either could be an error. The 465 acres of Possum Point between the public road and the beach were called Fickling's at confiscation and bought by W. D. Brown, in April 1876, along with adjacent property totaling 1000 acres. The Federal government recorded Brown's bid of $150 as highest offered. Just a year before his murder, Brown sold the 465 acre Fickling plot for $10,000 to Roy Rainey. The rest went in plots of 100 to 165 acres, all eventually picked up by Thorne and Loomis. The Shipyard plot, part of which was also described as Fickling's by islanders was acquired in 1867 by John E. White, who purchased it from the government for $725. He was evidently acting as agent for Elisha C. White to whom he deeded it for the above price. The 1765 acres were sold back to John's wife Mary for $10,000 and sold by her to Jedediah Dwelle for the same amount in 1871. Twenty years later Clyde paid over three times that sum, as well as Dwelle's unpaid taxes. Clyde sold to Rainey and he to Thorne and Loomis.

6. GARDNER. *Gardner's* (1424A.) A large plantation of 1424 acres on the north side of Broad Creek, bounded east by Marshlands and Sand Hill, west by Otter Hole and north by Pineland Tract and Hanahan's, was referred to in con-

fiscation reports as Gardner's. It was very probably the
former home of Charles Davant, murdered at Two Oaks
in Revolutionary War days, but a part was referred to as Col.
Garden's in a boundary listing of 1795. Since it was sold
by the Federal government to the Sea Island Cotton Co. it
was not redeemable by Gardner heirs. The United States
Cotton Co. then bought it and sold it to J. L. Dimmock who
sold some of it to Negroes and most of it W. L. Hurley.
March Gardner did make some claims for land and his son
Gabriel P. Gardner, postmaster 1882-86, bought part of
Fish Haul. Gabriel's wife Susan and daughter Sarah kept
the land, but granddaughter Eugenia Gardner Heyward let
it be sold for delinquent taxes. Roy Rainey picked it up and
sold it to Thorne and Loomis.

7. GRAHAM. *Honey Horn* (1120A). William J. Graham,
already owner of a large estate on the mainland at Grahamville, bought Honey Horn from the Stoneys, who had acquired it from the estate of John Hanahan in 1805. The
plantation properly included lot No. 11, 270 acres bounded
by Muddy and Crooked (Jarvis) Creeks, as well as 850
acres between Broad Creek and the Atlantic, bounded north
by Leamington and south by Shipyard. Hanahan's will
mentioned furniture from his house on Hilton Head, but
where it was located is not known. The Graham house on
the old Bayley Barony lot No. 11 was only partly finished
when Fort Walker fell, and although this would later be
known as the Honey Horn Big House, the Grahams evidently never lived there. The 1861 map prepared for Sherman shows the name Graham beside a house on Skull Creek
north of Widow Stoney's. Perhaps it was their temporary
home while waiting for the new house to be completed.
Freeman Dodd bought Honey Horn from the government
in 1863 for $200 and sold it for $10,000 to Ramon Rivas.
Therefore the land was unredeemable by Graham heirs,
although when the Valentines bought it in 1870 they asked
Graham for a quit-claim, thus acknowledging his prewar
title. No such recognition was given by previous purchasers,
as Tomas Quinteres and Rafael Alvarez bought half the
land from Rivas and all sold out to Ana and Robustrand

Hergues at tremendous profit. Valentines lost Honey Horn in 1884 when Witte Brothers foreclosed their mortgage and sold the estate to F. R. Klem. Klem sold off some small plots to Negroes and the rest to Clyde in 1889. From Clyde ownership went to Rainey and then to Thorne and Loomis. Somewhere along the line the 850 acres on the ocean front were sold separately from lot No. 11 and apparently were known as Dilling's or the Hill Place. Later they were mistakenly considered part of Leamington.

8. JENKINS. *Jenkins' Island.* (315A). Although Jenkins Island is the name remaining on today's maps, this island between Skull and Crooked (Jarvis) Creeks was evidently in the original Bayley grant and bought by John Gascoigne in June 1729. It was called John's Island on maps of 1777 and Pope's on the Navy map of 1873. Part of it has been called Hogg or Hog Island, and a Hogg family were residents of the parish in early days. The Jenkins family owned land on St. Helena and Hilton Head, and the Daniel Jenkins who sold Drayton part of his pineland tract may also have been the owner of the island that bears his name. Sherman's map of 1861 shows several buildings on it, but records no name of the residents. Nothing else has been found to indicate owners prior to 1900.

9. KIRK. *Cherry Hill* (400A). The Kirk name is the most frequent inscribed on the gravestones of Zion Chapel cemetery. Dr. James Kirk's headstone was the last erected there, July 31, 1858. Two Kirk brothers, John and Rollin, were among the Confederates who made successful raids on the Yankee-held island in wartime. There is some indication, but not actual proof, that their residence on Hilton Head was the plantation called Cherry Hill, sold in 1876 to W. D. Brown, who also acquired Possum Point and Folly Field. The price Brown paid for Cherry Hill was $400. He sold one acre each to Negro Baptists and Methodists for their churches. After Brown's murder, the land was sold to Roy Rainey, with the exception of 51 acres owned for a few years by the Osprey Fishing Club. Thorne and Loomis took over from both.

10. LAWTON. *Calibogue* (1820A) Joseph Lawton mar-

ried Martha Sarah Stoney Barksdale, widow of Thomas
H. Barksdale, in 1836 and thereby acquired rights for himself and his heirs to both Barksdale and Stoney property
mentioned in the marriage settlement. The heirs were
Samuel Lawton, son of Martha and Joseph, and an adopted
daughter Josephine Polhill, and they were able to regain
the land under the Redemption Act. Samuel was forced
to sell it, however, to pay the mortgage, and Hariett B.
Lawton bought it at public auction in 1889. She sold it to
Clyde for a small profit, and Thorne and Loomis became
owners in 1931. The land included a marshy wooded area
that has been marked "Sanctuary" on maps of Colonial
times and is still a wild-life refuge.

11. MATHEWS. *Sand Hill* (600A), *Folly Field* (500A).
The Reverend Philip Mathews and his wife Rebecca Da-
vant owned two plantations. Both plots were often called
"Mathews' Land." W. D. Brown bought the 500 acres of
Folly Field for $110 on the same April day in 1876 when
he acquired Possum Point and Cherry Hill. Part of Sand
Hill had been included with Marshlands in a government
surveyor's error and sold to Negroes, so only 200 acres
were redeemable by Mathews heirs on July 10, 1874.
These heirs were two daughters and evidently a daughter-
in-law of Rebecca and Philip Mathews: Sarah Mathews
Lawton (Mrs. W. G.); Mary E. Mathews George, whose
husband was a clergyman; Widow Mary Lawton, who
must have been the widow of son Theodore. They sold
the Mathews land to Clyde and ownership passed from
him to Rainey and then to Thorne and Loomis.

12. POPES. *Cotton Hope.* (1000A), *Coggins Point* (803A),
Point Comfort (1750A), *Leamington* (2000A), *Piney
Woods or Pineland* (1000A). The Pope family is one of
the most numerous, rivalling the Kirks, and certainly held
the most acreage at Secession, with ownership being divided
among sons, cousins and brothers. They also owned The
Oaks on St. Helena, Violet Bank near Bluffton, Haig's
Point on Daufuskie and other property. The first Popes
on Hilton Head were probably William and Sarah, whose
son James was born here in 1786. In 1791 they sold 365

SIGNALING

BY

THE SEA

THE WHITE FLAG

WITH

THE RED CENTER

This station was established by Lieutenant E. J. Keenan on the roof of the mansion of a planter at the extreme northern point of Hilton Head Island, Port Royal Bay. Through this station were exchanged many messages between General W. T. Sherman and Admiral S. F. Dupont. Sherman had been forced by Savannah's stubborn resistance to prepare for siege operations against the city, and perfect coöperation between the army and navy became imperative. The signal station adjoining the one portrayed above was erected on the house formerly owned by John C. Calhoun, lying within sight of Fort Pulaski, at the mouth of the Savannah River. Late in December, General Hardee and his Confederate troops evacuated the city. Sherman was enabled to make President Lincoln a present of one of the last of the Southern strongholds.

FROM SHORE TO SHIP—HILTON HEAD SIGNAL STATION

Hilton Head Signal Station — *Review of Reviews*

Earth defenses at Fort Sherman. Part of the Federal
fortifications of the Fort Walker area.

Post Office (1952), showing a "Marsh Tacky" and its colt

acres of their Coggins Point land to the Scotts, keeping the 803 acres that would remain in the Pope family till confiscation. In 1793 Popes bought Lot No. 4 of Bayley's Barony and also owned Leamington. Point Comfort, also called Calibogue Plantation, was bought by William Pope from the heirs of John and James Davant in 1823 or 1824, probably in two transactions. Cotton Hope, sometimes called Skull Creek Plantation, also belonged to the Honorable William E. Pope and boasted a fine house whose tabby wall foundations still stand not far from the road to Seabrook Landing. The Honorable William was often called Squire Pope, and was referred to both as William Junior and William Senior (evidently before and after his father's death and also before and after the birth of his son William who died young, thereby causing some confusion as to which William was meant. William Pope property is given as one of the boundaries for the northern part of Fish Haul and evidently indicates the tract called Piney Woods or Pinelands. Both Joseph and James Pope are on record as island residents and Joseph was listed in the Thorne-Loomis accounts as owner of Leamington. Like Otter Hole and Muddy Creek Place, it was bought from the Federal government in wartime by the Sea Island Cotton Co. and was not redeemable by pre-war owners. Later a part was sold to Negroes and part to the Beaufort Gun Club, who sold to a North Carolina group. The government kept for itself enough acreage for a light-house, which it erected there in 1881, the site of Camp McDougal in World War II. Pinelands was bought by R. C. McIntire in 1876, who also took Fairfield, Seabrook and Grasslawn. Coggins Point was held as a military reservation till 1927, when it was sold by the Secretary of War, leaving only two Pope plantations redeemable by payment of the tax assessment. Sarah Lovinia Pope, widow of William, redeemed Point Comfort in 1872 and willed it to her daughter Eliza, wife of the Reverend Alsop Park Woodward. (Sarah's son William had died before his father). Lawyers acting for John E. Woodward, Eliza's son and heir, redeemed Cotton Hope in 1887. The heirs sold Cotton Hope in small plots to Negroes and in larger plots to Roy Rainey. Point Comfort went to Clyde in 1889. Both eventually went to Thorne and Loomis.

13. SEABROOK. *Seabrook's* (1500A). Although Seabrooks had long held property elsewhere in the area, they apparently did not come to Hilton Head till after 1800, possibly after 1820. William Seabrook bought the four plantations lying between Cotton Hope and Myrtle Bank formerly owned by the Fylers, Currels, Talbirds or Talbots and the Wallises or Wallaces. His heir, James Seabrook, was unable to redeem it under the Act of 1872 for lack of funds. R. C. McIntire bought it, promising James that he could buy it back whenever he had the money. In 1873 James deeded Seabrook Plantation to McIntire, apparently still unable to raise the small sum needed. After McIntire's death the land went to Clyde in 1895.

14. SCOTT. *Grasslawn* (600A). In 1791 William Scott bought 365 acres on the inland side of Coggins Point, and since William was a member of the Revolutionary War Partisan band stationed on Hilton Head, it is likely that he already owned land there. Joseph Scott was an island resident in 1799. Since their land lay next to Coggins Point it was likely the plantation called Grasslawn. The Scott name does not appear in the claims under the Redemption Act of 1872. Grasslawn was bought from the government on Feb. 12, 1876 by William Wilson, who got 400 acres for $90. The remaining 200 acres were kept by the government as a military reservation and may be the site marked Springfield on postwar maps. Wilson sold to R. C. McIntire three months later, and in 1895 McIntire heirs sold to Clyde, who bought the entire McIntire holdings of Grasslawn, Pinelands, Seabrook's and part of Fairfield.

15. STONEYS. *Fairfield* (350A), *Shipyard or Brickyard* (1765A), *Possum Point* (1000A), *Otter Hole* (422A), *Honey Horn* (1000A). John and James Stoney were early residents of the island and added to their property when John Hanahan's estate was for sale in 1805. They sold Otter Hole to the Stuarts and Honey Horn to Graham, but kept Fairfield, occupied at Secession by Colonel Joseph Stoney. The grave of Captain James Stoney (1772-1827)

lies on Fish Haul land next to the unmarked graves of John (Old Jack) and John Stafford Stoney. It is not known when they bought or sold Shipyard or Possum Point. Both had been sold by the Federal government after confiscation and were not redeemable. The report that Shipyard was once called Brickyard indicates that it may once have belonged to that brickmaking lighthouse builder, Henry Talbot-Talbird, before Stoneys took over. After confiscation part of Fairfield was bought by Henry and Alfred Hudson and inherited by James B. Hudson who was appointed Postmaster in 1923. At the same time (1876) several Negroes bought small plots and the balance of 350 acres went to R. C. McIntire for $530. His heirs sold it to F. R. Klem for $2000 in 1885. The McDonald-Wilkins Co. of Savannah leased the cotton fields from 1913 to 1932. Rainey picked up almost all of the land not owned by the Hudsons, who still live here, and sold it to Thorne and Loomis.

16. STUART. *Stuart. Otter Hole, or, Otter Hall.* (900A). John Allan Stuart was editor of the Charleston *Mercury* and waged the battle for States Rights on its editorial page. He and his family lived in Beaufort for many years in a house that later became the Sea Island Hotel. Their Hilton Head land was bought from John Stoney and lay on the northwest side of Broad Creek, between Gardner's and Muddy Creek Place. Along with Leamington, Gardner's and Muddy Creek it was bought in wartime by the Sea Island Cotton Company and sold to the United States Cotton Company in 1888. In 1896 the latter firm went bankrupt and Otter Hole was bought by the southerner, W. J. Verdier and later sold to F. E. Wilder, who in turn sold to W. L. Hurley, from whom it was purchased by Thorne and Loomis. The family name was sometimes spelled Stewart, and the plantation known as Stuart's or Stewart's.

17. WILLS or WELLS. Since Wills was on the map prepared for Sherman in 1861, the family may have been pre-war residents at Possum Point. The map contains errors, however. The 1825 map of Vignoles and Ravenel listed Wells, a well-known family in the parish in Colonial times.

18. WILSON. Wm. Wilson was post-war purchaser of Grasslawn, but whether he was pre-war owner is not known.

The above summary, with its unknowns and suppositions, its bargain tax sales and fabulous profits, redemptions, foreclosed mortgages, bankruptcies and the almost complete disappearing of Southern ante-bellum owners is a fitting conclusion to a chapter on war's aftermath. For the old-time landholders there was no hope for the future on Hilton Head.

CHAPTER IX

A NEW
BEGINNING

C HANGING TIMES and plans finally persuaded Thorne and Loomis to begin selling their island domain. On December 20, 1949, Fred C. Hack, a young lumberman from Hinesville, Georgia, learned that the south end of Hilton Head was for sale. Shortly thereafter he made an inspection trip accompanied by General J. B. Fraser and Mr. C. C. Stebbins and all succumbed to the island's enchantment at first sight. Not only could they see a profit to be made from the lumbering of the island's yellow pine timber but—more important—they understood how the logging could be accomplished without destroying the wild loveliness of woodland and marsh. An option was secured, prepared for Thorne and Loomis by Mr. Knoth, and by the end of March 1950 this southern part of the island was owned by The Hilton Head Company, a corporation organized for the purpose.

Development of a portion of the Hilton Head Company purchase would later be handled by the Sea Pines Plantation Company and associates, whose principal owners and managers are Charles E. Fraser, James C. Self and T. L. Caudle, III.

In May of 1951 another company was formed by O. T. McIntosh, C. C. Stebbins and Fred C. Hack to purchase land on the northern end of the island. Their corporation was named Honey Horn Plantation and it continues to operate as such. (Several other companies have been organized to aid in handling the development of the island. One very active company has been Hilton Head Real Estate Company, a sales company, organized by J. Wilton Graves. Mr. Graves, a member of the South Carolina House of Representatives, has contributed a great deal to the development through legislation sponsored by him.)

At first the only way to reach the island was by boat, and among those in service was *The Alligator,* which was finally left to rot on the shores of Spanish Wells. In 1953 the South Carolina State Highway Department opened a ferry service operating between Buckingham landing and the dock on Jenkins Island. Several cars or trucks could be carried each trip and a road bridged the marshy ground between Jenkins Island and the rest of Hilton Head. The barge *Gay Time* began the service early in 1953 but was soon replaced by a power-driven ferry, the *Pocahontas.* Even with the increased accommodations of the *Pocahontas* many a car was left behind on Sunday evenings as the ferry pulled away on her last trip to the main land. Going down to the dock to count the left-overs became a regular summer Sunday evening pastime. More and more homes were being built on the island. A public health center was opened on the main road next to the post office and electric power was installed. A new beginning was indeed underway.

From the day Fred Hack first saw the island he kept always in mind this dream of a new beginning for Hilton Head. He and his associates wanted to give full sway to the island's natural beauty, emphasize its historic past, bring in all the modern conveniences that would aid its future happiness and then make Hilton Head easy of access so that many others could come and share its fascination.

In keeping with his wish to preserve wild life, he welcomed back a group of scientists sponsored by the University of South Carolina who had already begun a survey of island plant and animal life. So far two new subspecies have been identified for the first time: the island raccoon, *procyon lotor solutus,* described by Nelson and Goldman, and the island white-tailed deer, *odocoilous virginianus hiltonensis,* described by Goldman and Kellogg. Additional new sub-species may come to light as the work goes on to completion when funds are available. Although limited hunting has been allowed on the island, there has always been an effort to preserve the sanctuary and in time perhaps the island will become a wild-life refuge. It is indeed a near paradise for bird lovers, and the list of birds to be seen on Hilton Head include the pileated woodpecker, painted bunting, night herons, cattle egrets, a host of songbirds, shorebirds, water-fowl, hawks and owls, both those that only pass by in migration and those that make the island a permanent home. For fishermen it offers equal plenty with sea bass, whiting, winter trout, sheepshead and other varieties ready to take the lure.

Since 1950 Fred Hack and his entire family have made the island their permanent home, remodeling and enlarging one of the houses at Honey Horn. Like their predecessors they have done a great deal of delving into the past, a past whose historic interest they hope to preserve and cherish without losing sight of Hilton Head's future and the dream they have for its new beginning. Their home has become a treasure store of island relics: the giant-sized fossil tooth of a prehistoric mastodon unearthed by island roadbuilders, an ancient canoe, Indian pottery fragments and shell tools, old coins, handblown bottles, stoneware jugs, inkwells, uniform buttons, old maps, diaries, newspaper clippings. There are treasures of the future, also: plans for new roads, names of streets and boulevards, shopping areas, a medical center and first sketches of the new bridge to the mainland.

The bridge is one part of the dream that has come to fulfillment, and with the aid and counsel of the company directors and the enthusiastic assistance of their staffs, everyone is sure that the rest will follow. The bridge with its two spans, one between the mainland and Pinckney Island over Mackay Creek and the other between Pinckney and Hilton Head over Skull Creek, was completed under a three-man commission. It was dedicated on May 19, 1956, as the James F. Byrnes Crossing. Representatives of the United States Army and Navy, the Coast Guard, Air Force and Marine Corps were all there to give salute. If ghosts walk anywhere on this green earth, there was surely another delegation in Confederate gray. Perhaps, also, an invisible Spanish caravel dipped sail in Skull Creek, while the wrath of Captain Hilton paced the deck of his English ship *Adventure* and peered through a ghostly spyglass at his namesake island. The past touches hands with the future on Hilton Head.

SELECTED BIBLIOGRAPHY

Swanton, John R. *Early History of the Creek Indians and Their Neighbors*. U. S. Printing Office, 1922

Lowery, Woodbury. *Spanish Settlements within the Present Limits of the United States*. 2 vols. Putnam, 1905.

Bolton, Herbert E. *Arrendondo's Historical Proof of Spain's Title to Georgia*. U. of California Press, 1925.

Winsor, Justin. *Narrative and Critical History of America*. Houghton, Mifflin, 1886.

Lorant, Stefan. *The New World*. Duell, Sloane & Pearce, 1946.

Crane, Verner, W. *The Southern Frontier*. Duke University Press, 1928.

Elliott, William. *Carolina Sports by Land and Water*. Charleston, 1848.

Johnson, Guy G. *A Social History of the Sea Islands*. University of North Carolina Press, 1930.

The Georgia Historical Quarterly.

The South Carolina Historical and Genealogical Magazine.

The South Carolina Historical Collections.

Salley, Alexander. *Narratives Early Carolina*. Scribners, 1911.

Jones, Samuell. *Siege of Charleston*. Neale Publishing Co. New York, 1911.

Macartney, C. E. *Mr. Lincoln's Admirals*. Funk and Wagnalls, 1956.

Miller, F. T. (ed). *Photographic History of the Civil War*. (10 vols.). *Review of Reviews*, 1911.

Lee, Fitzhugh (ed). *The American Soldier in our Civil War*. Frank Leslie's Illustrated Magazine," 1895.

Weld, Stephen. *Letters and Diary*. Riverside Press, 1912.

Andrews, Elizabeth H. *Charles Howard Family Domestic History*. Privately printed, 1956. Cambridge, Mass.

Abstract of Titles. Honey Horn Plantation, Hilton Head Co., 1951.

Official Records of the War of the Rebellion (27 vols.). Series I, volumes VI, XIV, LIII, Series III; volumes II, III.

Mills, Robert. Historical Atlas of South Carolina. Facsimile reprint of maps, Bostick & Thornely, Columbia, S. C. 1937.

Beaufort County. Map No. 87155, Bureau of Navy Yards and Docks. Drawn by Law & Kirk, 1873.

Map of the Country surrounding Port Royal, compiled for Brig.-Gen. T. W. Sherman, November 1861. Internal Revenue Service, Record Group 58, Cartographic Records Branch, National Archives and Records Service Washington 25, D. C. (Map I-28).

Map of the city of Hilton Head, April, 1864 (Map I 33-I). Same source as preceding item.

ACKNOWLEDGEMENTS

For gracious help and encouragement in writing this book, my grateful thanks to my husband, Lloyd E. Holmgren, and daughter Karen; to Mr. and Mrs. Fred C. Hack, Mr. Orion D. Hack, Mrs. Phyllis L. Stone, Mrs. Wade Hines and the Rev. Robert E. H. Peeples of Hilton Head Island.

For special aid in research my deep appreciation to Hardin Davant (Mrs. John) Hanahan of Knoxville, Tennessee, whose unpublished collection of genealogical data supplied much valuable information.

For additional aid in research my thanks to Miss Elizabeth H. Andrews of Cambridge, Massachusetts, for her history of the Howard family; Mr. J. G. Gemmell for recollections of Hilton Head; Mrs. Foreman M. Hawes of the Georgia Historical Society in Savannah and the Colonial Dames Collection there; Miss Margaret Godley of the Savannah Public Library; the public library of Ridgeland, South Carolina; the South Carolina Historicl Society in Columbia and in Charleston; Miss Mabel Runette of the Township Library, Mrs. Nellie Fripp of the Historical Museum and the Rev. John Hardy of St. Helena Church, all of Beaufort, South Carolina; the Rt. Rev. Albert S. Thomas of Wadmalaw Island, South Carolina; the Rev. John Blackburn of West Columbia, S. C.; Mrs. Alan Laird Jervey of Richmond, Virginia; F. W. Bradley of Columbia, S. C.; Henry P. Kendall of Camden, S. C.; Mrs. Samuell M. Hasell and J. Ross Hanahan of Charleston, S. C.; Mrs. Robert Hartzog of St. Matthews, S. C.; Mr. and Mrs. Lawrence W. Baynard and Mr. and Mrs. Frank J. Dana of St. Petersburg, Florida; Mrs. Gustave A. Kalber, Hartsville, S. C., and the many divisions of the National Archives and Records Service, the Department of the Army, Navy, Post Office, Treasury and the Library of Congress in Washington, D. C.